MALCOLM·HILLIER'S
CHRISTMAS

MALCOLM·HILLIER'S
CHRISTMAS

Photography by
DIANA MILLER

DORLING KINDERSLEY
LONDON • NEW YORK • STUTTGART

A DORLING KINDERSLEY BOOK

PROJECT EDITOR Susan Thompson
ART EDITOR Pauline Bayne
MANAGING EDITOR Mary-Clare Jerram
MANAGING ART EDITOR Gill Della Casa
PRODUCTION CONTROLLER Meryl Silbert

First published in Great Britain in 1992
by Dorling Kindersley Limited,
9 Henrietta Street, London WC2E 8PS

Visit us on the World Wide Web at
http://www.dk.com

A CIP catalogue record for this book is available from
the British Library.

ISBN 0 7513 05383

Typeset by The Cooling Brown Partnership, London
Text film output by The Right Type, London
Reproduced by Colourscan, Singapore
Printed and bound by Arti Grafiche, Italy

CONTENTS

INTRODUCTION

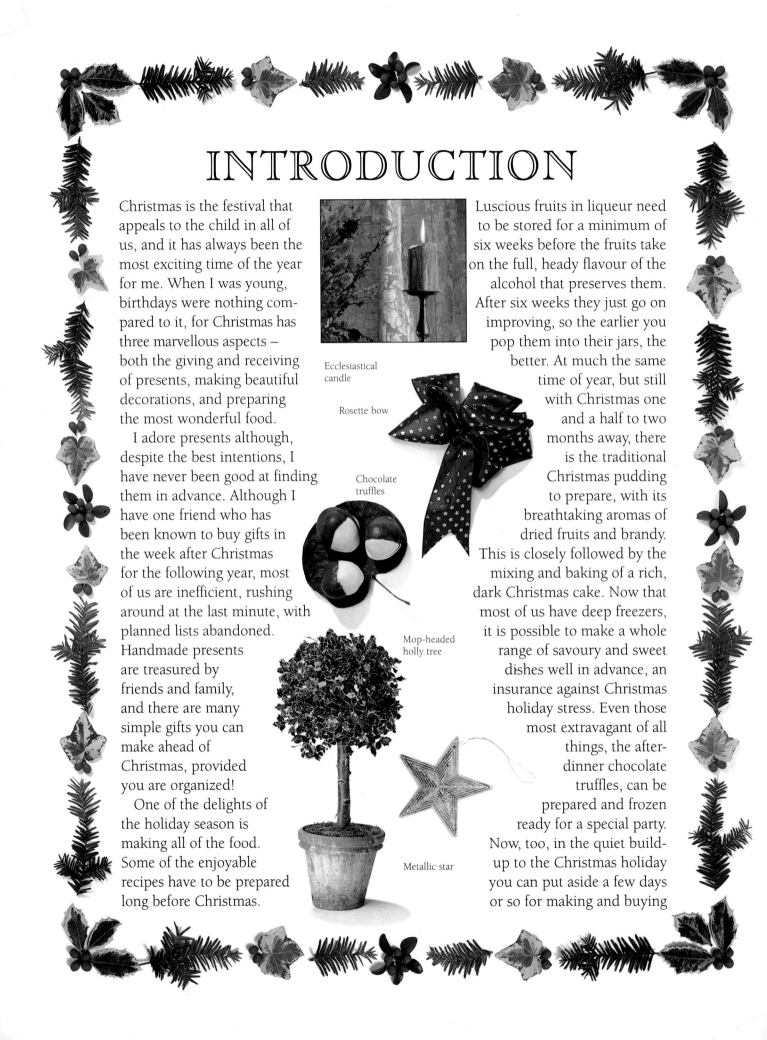

Christmas is the festival that appeals to the child in all of us, and it has always been the most exciting time of the year for me. When I was young, birthdays were nothing compared to it, for Christmas has three marvellous aspects – both the giving and receiving of presents, making beautiful decorations, and preparing the most wonderful food.

I adore presents although, despite the best intentions, I have never been good at finding them in advance. Although I have one friend who has been known to buy gifts in the week after Christmas for the following year, most of us are inefficient, rushing around at the last minute, with planned lists abandoned. Handmade presents are treasured by friends and family, and there are many simple gifts you can make ahead of Christmas, provided you are organized!

One of the delights of the holiday season is making all of the food. Some of the enjoyable recipes have to be prepared long before Christmas.

Ecclesiastical candle

Rosette bow

Chocolate truffles

Mop-headed holly tree

Metallic star

Luscious fruits in liqueur need to be stored for a minimum of six weeks before the fruits take on the full, heady flavour of the alcohol that preserves them. After six weeks they just go on improving, so the earlier you pop them into their jars, the better. At much the same time of year, but still with Christmas one and a half to two months away, there is the traditional Christmas pudding to prepare, with its breathtaking aromas of dried fruits and brandy. This is closely followed by the mixing and baking of a rich, dark Christmas cake. Now that most of us have deep freezers, it is possible to make a whole range of savoury and sweet dishes well in advance, an insurance against Christmas holiday stress. Even those most extravagant of all things, the after-dinner chocolate truffles, can be prepared and frozen ready for a special party. Now, too, in the quiet build-up to the Christmas holiday you can put aside a few days or so for making and buying decorations for the tree and house. Make the most of dried flowers, for they are at their very best in the autumn and winter in the Northern hemisphere. Of course, those who live in the Southern hemisphere will enjoy the bountiful summer flowers available to them.

The focal decoration for Christmas must be the tree. Children are thrilled by it and I suspect that it still holds great magic for all of us. Prince Albert introduced the custom to England by bringing cut conifers from Germany in the nineteenth century. These were the spruce trees that drop their needles within a few days of being cut. Despite this, I am still very fond of them: their aromatic scent always transports me back to my childhood and to the wild hope that there might be snow outside on Christmas Day. Christmas tree production is today a booming business, and varieties that hold their needles and have a good, full shape are readily available. I favour these but, despite their keeping qualities, I still decorate the tree and put up the decorations just three or four days before Christmas.

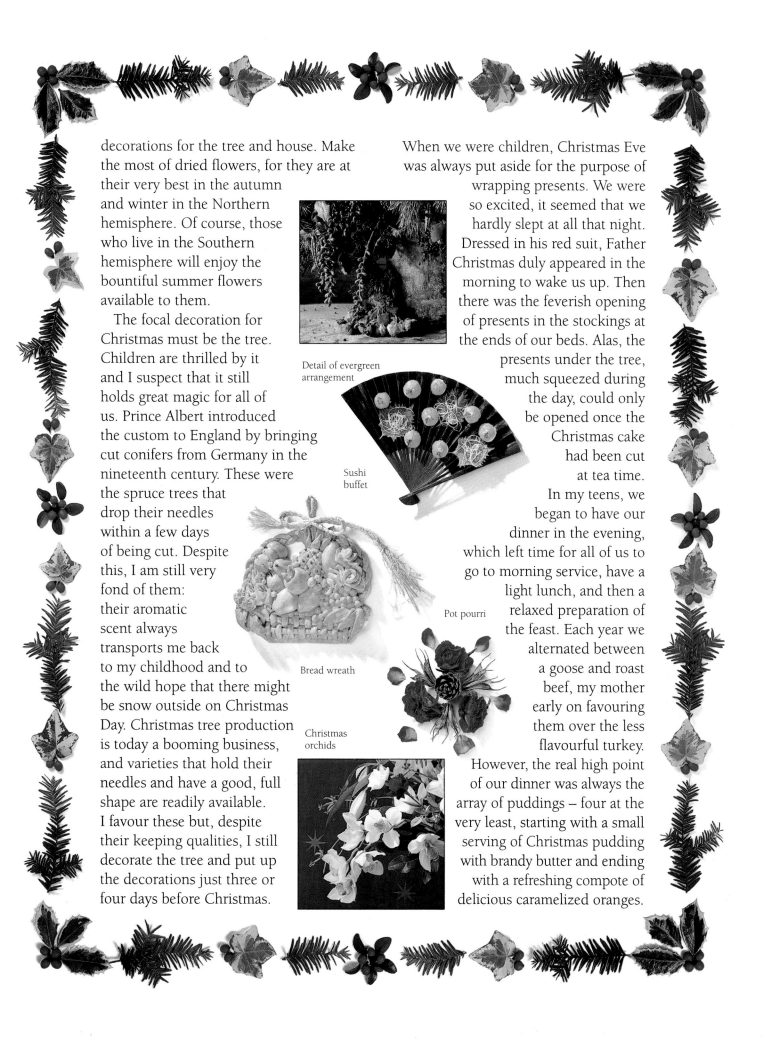

Detail of evergreen arrangement

Sushi buffet

Bread wreath

Christmas orchids

Pot pourri

When we were children, Christmas Eve was always put aside for the purpose of wrapping presents. We were so excited, it seemed that we hardly slept at all that night. Dressed in his red suit, Father Christmas duly appeared in the morning to wake us up. Then there was the feverish opening of presents in the stockings at the ends of our beds. Alas, the presents under the tree, much squeezed during the day, could only be opened once the Christmas cake had been cut at tea time. In my teens, we began to have our dinner in the evening, which left time for all of us to go to morning service, have a light lunch, and then a relaxed preparation of the feast. Each year we alternated between a goose and roast beef, my mother early on favouring them over the less flavourful turkey. However, the real high point of our dinner was always the array of puddings – four at the very least, starting with a small serving of Christmas pudding with brandy butter and ending with a refreshing compote of delicious caramelized oranges.

Chapter One

EARLY PREPARATIONS

Two months before Christmas, it takes
will-power to start preparing gifts, decorations,
and food for the big day, but it is well worth it.
Finishing some jobs early, and planning the rest,
makes life so much easier in the hectic days that
lead up to Christmas. You can make imaginative
presents of pot pourri, paper decorations,
candles, dried-flower arangements, luscious
liqueur fruits, Christmas puddings, and a truly
spectacular cake while there is still plenty
of time to work at your leisure.

Glowing Dried Display
A golden bundle of lichen-covered larch
twigs, seeding grasses, deep red roses, and Chinese
lanterns split open to form flowers stand without
a vase. Old rope, sprayed gold, holds it together,
and gilded pomegranates lie at the base.

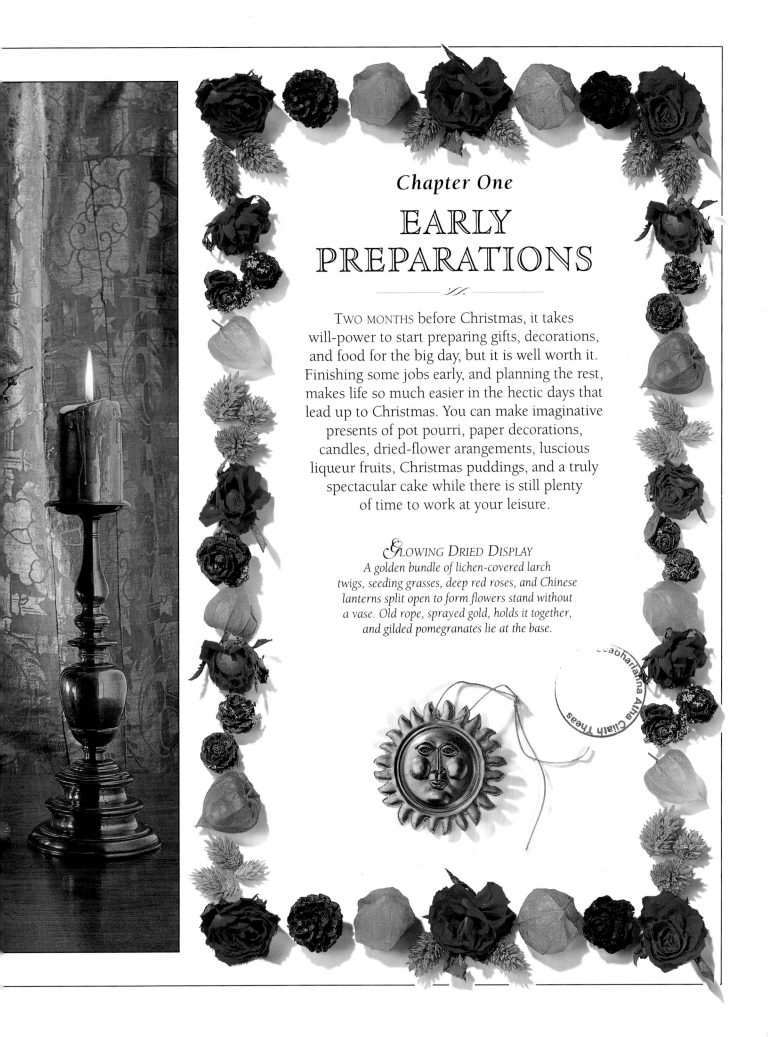

Scented Gifts

CUSHIONS AND SACHETS make wonderful Christmas presents, especially if you use rich, festive-looking materials, such as velvet or brocade. They are very easy to make, although you may prefer to buy ready-made cushion covers and simply insert a sachet of pot pourri between the cover and the filling. Spicy citrus pomanders – also easy-to-make gifts – offer another way to perfume a room, their exotic fragrance lasting for years.

Glass sphere

Perfumed Pillows
Fill a flat muslin bag with a handful of fine pot pourri, and sew it to the inside of a cushion cover to make a delicately scented pillow. You can easily renew the pot pourri from time to time.

Glass Pomanders
The beauty of glass pomanders is that you can enjoy the fragrance of the pot pourri for longer than if it were displayed in an open container, and still see it through the glass. This pot pourri is made of fragrant rose petals, other flowers, and spices.

Red, tare ribbon

Dried rose

Decorative edging

Rosy Pomander
A muslin sphere is tightly packed with rose pot pourri, and decorated with pink, red, and yellow, dried roses. To preserve the colours of the roses, hang the pomander away from direct sunlight.

CITRUS POMANDERS
Smelling deliciously of cloves and citrus zest, these pomanders are straightforward to make yourself (SEE PAGE 32).

Braiding •

SCENTED TASSEL
When I had to restitch this antique tassel, I put a tablespoon of rosemary-scented pot pourri in its padded centre to make it fragrant.

Piping•

FRAGRANT SACHETS
To create these small sachets, either place some pot pourri in the centre of a circle of fabric and gather the edges with ribbon, or make mini-cushions with piped edges.

Tassel •

POT POURRIS

DELICIOUSLY PERFUMED pot pourris make a perfect present. Mix your own dry or moist pot pourris from fresh flowers to create more subtle and delicate fragrances than those of commercial pot pourris. The early recipes never exuded the powerful aromas of the pot pourris on sale now, and why should they? A room needs only the gentlest scent of flowers and spices to give it a special, indefinable charm.

CHRISTMAS POT POURRI
(Moist method)

*1 litre (2 pt) partially dried,
  deep red rose petals*
300 g (10 oz) coarse salt
250 ml (½ pt) preserved ivy leaves
250 ml (½ pt) dried moss
125 ml (¼ pt) Nigella orientalis seedheads
20 small pine cones
4 tbs dried juniper berries, lightly crushed
2 tbs fresh or dried mint
2 tbs ground cinnamon
2 tbs gum benzoin
4 drops lemon geranium oil
3 drops pine oil
2 drops rose oil

BLUE FLOWER POT POURRI
(Dry method)

*1 litre (2 pt) dried blue flowers, such as
  larkspur, delphiniums, and hydrangeas*
*500 ml (1 pt) dried lemon
  verbena leaves*
*250 ml (½ pt) dried eucalyptus
  leaves, flowers, and seeds*
250 ml (½ pt) oak moss
2 tbs ground orris root
4 drops carnation oil

Red rose petal

Pine cone

Preserved ivy leaf

Nigella orientalis seedhead

Chamomile flower

Dried hops

Marigold

DRY METHOD

Mixing by the dry method makes an attractive pot pourri, although the scent is not as strong as those made by the moist method. Mix dried, fragrant, flower petals, dried herbs, spices, a few drops of essential oils, and a fixative, such as vetiver, ground orris root, gum benzoin, tonka beans, or frankincense. Seal in a jar, and shake every day for 8 weeks, to blend the fragrances.

LATE SUMMER POT POURRI
(Dry method)

500 ml (1 pt) dried, yellow rose petals
250 ml (½ pt) dried marigolds
250 ml (½ pt) dried hops
250 ml (½ pt) dried chamomile flowers
1 tbs ground orris root
4 drops rose oil
4 drops bergamot oil

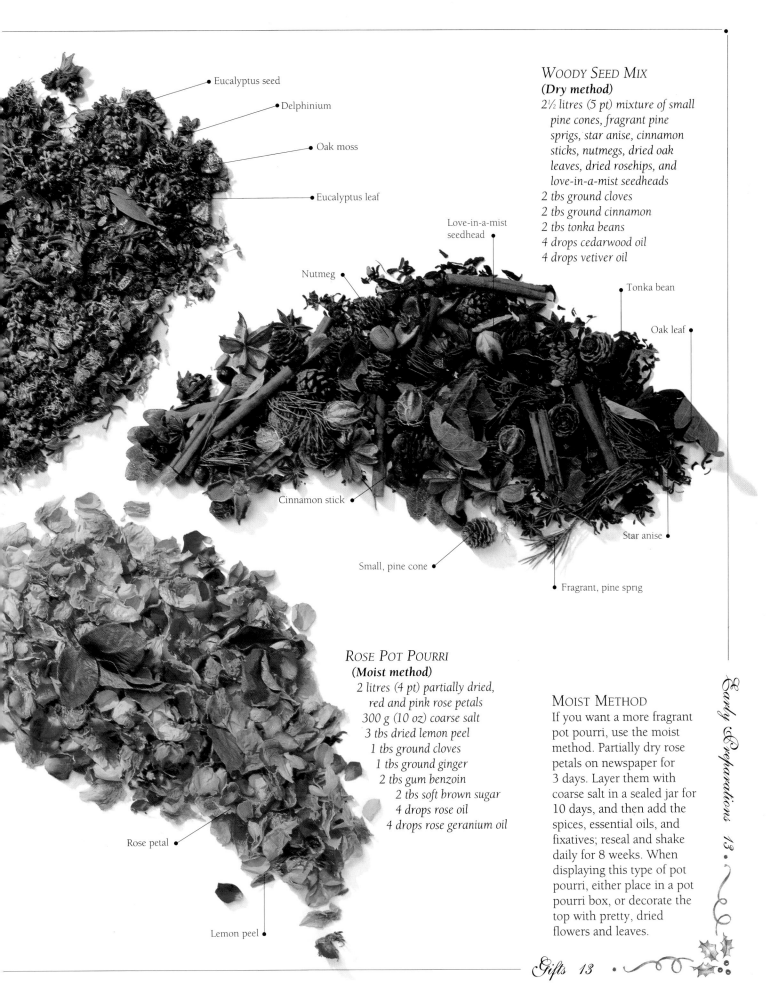

Eucalyptus seed

Delphinium

Oak moss

Eucalyptus leaf

WOODY SEED MIX
(Dry method)
2½ litres (5 pt) mixture of small
   pine cones, fragrant pine
   sprigs, star anise, cinnamon
   sticks, nutmegs, dried oak
   leaves, dried rosehips, and
   love-in-a-mist seedheads
2 tbs ground cloves
2 tbs ground cinnamon
2 tbs tonka beans
4 drops cedarwood oil
4 drops vetiver oil

Love-in-a-mist
seedhead

Nutmeg

Tonka bean

Oak leaf

Cinnamon stick

Star anise

Small, pine cone

Fragrant, pine sprig

ROSE POT POURRI
(Moist method)
2 litres (4 pt) partially dried,
   red and pink rose petals
300 g (10 oz) coarse salt
3 tbs dried lemon peel
1 tbs ground cloves
1 tbs ground ginger
2 tbs gum benzoin
2 tbs soft brown sugar
4 drops rose oil
4 drops rose geranium oil

MOIST METHOD
If you want a more fragrant
pot pourri, use the moist
method. Partially dry rose
petals on newspaper for
3 days. Layer them with
coarse salt in a sealed jar for
10 days, and then add the
spices, essential oils, and
fixatives; reseal and shake
daily for 8 weeks. When
displaying this type of pot
pourri, either place in a pot
pourri box, or decorate the
top with pretty, dried
flowers and leaves.

Rose petal

Lemon peel

Early Preparations 13.

Fiery Fruit Candles

THE MENTION OF CHRISTMAS brings several images
to mind – a traditional wreath on the front door,
decorated Christmas trees, rich puddings, candle
light, a roaring fire, and a country cottage with
smoke curling out of the chimney, snugly nestling
between rolling fields blanketed in the crispest,
pure white snow. The last scene is not always
possible but the other images are quite easy
to achieve in reality. Filling the home with
candles creates an extra special atmosphere.
They are soft, yet intensely beautiful, giving
the light of atmosphere rather than the light
of practicality. They are warm and welcoming,
kind, and exciting, too. An arrangement
of fruit candles combined with real fruit
in a decorative basket forms
an unusual and beautiful
decoration, which you
could also give as a
present. A similar
basket filled with
eggs and egg candles
would make another
novel display or gift.

Apple candle

Candle of grapes

Elaeagnus leaf

WHAT YOU NEED
28 ml (1 oz) cooking oil
4 fruit moulds
Darning needle
Four 25 cm (10 in) wicks
*Four 13 cm (5 in) squares
of cardboard*
4 glasses
4 sticks
570 g (20 oz) paraffin wax
Cooking thermometer
*Orange, yellow, and
green dyes*
Citronella scent
Wicker basket
Real fruit

Orange

Lemon

MOULDED FRUIT CANDLES

MAKE ORANGE, LEMON, APPLE, and grape candles from moulds, then display them with real fruit.

1 Oil the mould. Thread the needle with the wick. Pierce the top of the mould from the inside. Thread through the wick, leaving 2.5 cm (1 in) at the top and 10 cm (4 in) at the open end.

2 Cut a collar from a cardboard square to support the mould. Place over a glass. Tie a stick to the wick and wind until taut. Heat the wax to 82° C (180° F) and add dye and scent. Fill the mould. Top up with wax after half an hour.

3 When completely cool, peel the mould off the candle. Cut the wick level at the base, and trim the top of the wick, leaving 1 cm (⅜ in) to light. Arrange in a wicker basket with real fruit.

Wicker basket

ℬASKET OF FRUIT
Create a spectacular centrepiece: a basket of lemons, oranges, apples, and grapes – some real, some in the form of candles. Make several candles of each fruit so that you can replace them as they burn down, thus ensuring a display that looks its best on several occasions.

CHORUS OF CANDLES

A FLOTILLA OF COLOURFUL, SCENTED CANDLES floating in a clear glass bowl, their sparkling flames reflecting in the water, makes a glowing table centrepiece. Fresh flowers or leaves add a finishing touch to the arrangement. On a windowsill in the same room, line up candles in old, terracotta pots or candles in tall glasses resembling festive, ice-cream sundaes. If you make the candles well in advance, all you have to do on Christmas Day is arrange them and light them.

Floating candle •

Holly leaf •

FIRE ON WATER
Candles seem to shine more brightly when floating in water, especially if they are grouped in a clear or cut-glass bowl, so the flames reflect off the glass and water. Candles with flat tops and rounded bases float best.

• Glass bowl
filled with water

Candle in a Flower Pot or Glass
WHAT YOU NEED
1 old terracotta pot or tall glass
570 g (20 oz) paraffin wax
Wick
1 stick or pencil
Cooking thermometer
Colouring
Fragrance

CANDLES IN GLASSES

Make candles in tall glass tumblers with two or three layers of different coloured wax to create decorative and safe lights for a table, mantelpiece, or shelf. Allow each layer of wax to solidify before adding the next.

MOULDED CANDLES

PRIME THE WICKS (STEP 1) for homemade candles. Don't choose too thick a wick or it will smoke.

1 Tie a length of wick, measuring about 2.5 cm (1 in) longer than the candle mould or container, to a stick or a pencil. Paint melted wax on to the wick and pull it straight. Leave it to set.

2 Suspend the wick inside the mould. Trim so that it almost touches the base of the mould or container. Heat the wax to 82° C (180° F), and add the colouring and fragrance. Pour into the mould. When solid, trim the wick to 1cm (⅜in).

• Glass tumbler with layers of different-coloured wax

FLOWER POT CANDLES

Old, straight-sided, terracotta pots make excellent containers for candles. Before you pour in the wax, make sure the pots are clean, and block the drainage holes with adhesive clay or plasticine. Add a drop of your favourite fragrance to the wick to give the candles a scent.

Terracotta pot •

Early Preparations 18 ·

PATTERNED TISSUE PAPER

MUCH OF THE WRAPPING PAPER available in shops is very expensive, and often rather boring. I prefer to make my own, using humble tissue paper. Inexpensive, it comes in an enormous range of vibrant colours, and is simple to decorate. I am especially partial to gold and silver patterns. They shine like jewels around the base of the Christmas tree, making presents look even more enticing. When clothed in a shining wrap and decorated with festive bows (SEE PAGES 96–97), even the simplest gift takes on a mysterious aura.

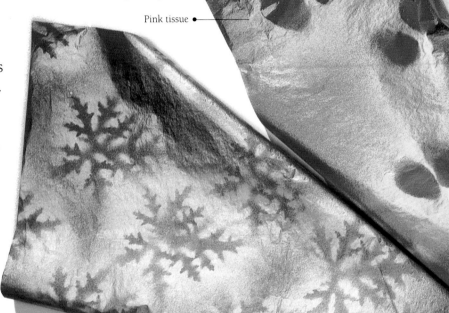

Stencil pattern from Brazil nuts

Pink tissue

STENCILLED PATTERNS
Delicate geranium leaves and large Brazil nuts provide the stencils for these patterned papers, although you can use any interestingly shaped forms. Simply place the objects on the paper and spray with gold, silver, or coloured paint. Use more than one colour if you wish.

TISSUE-PAPER DESIGNS

WHEN YOU SPRAY PAINT tissue paper, place it in a long, cardboard box, preferably outdoors.

✂ PLEATED PAPER ✂

1 *Pleat a sheet of tissue paper. Place in a long box and spray the silver paint from one side, at an angle, so that it catches only one edge of the pleats.*

2 *When dry, flatten the tissue paper and make another set of pleats at right angles to the first set. Spray paint again.*

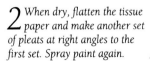

✂ TIE-DYE EFFECT ✂

1 *Make small, irregular twists all over a piece of tissue paper, and then loosely crumple the entire sheet.*

2 *Apply spray paint lightly and unevenly over the crumpled paper. When it is completely dry, flatten the tissue to use.*

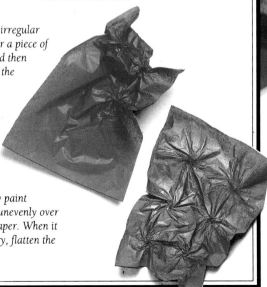

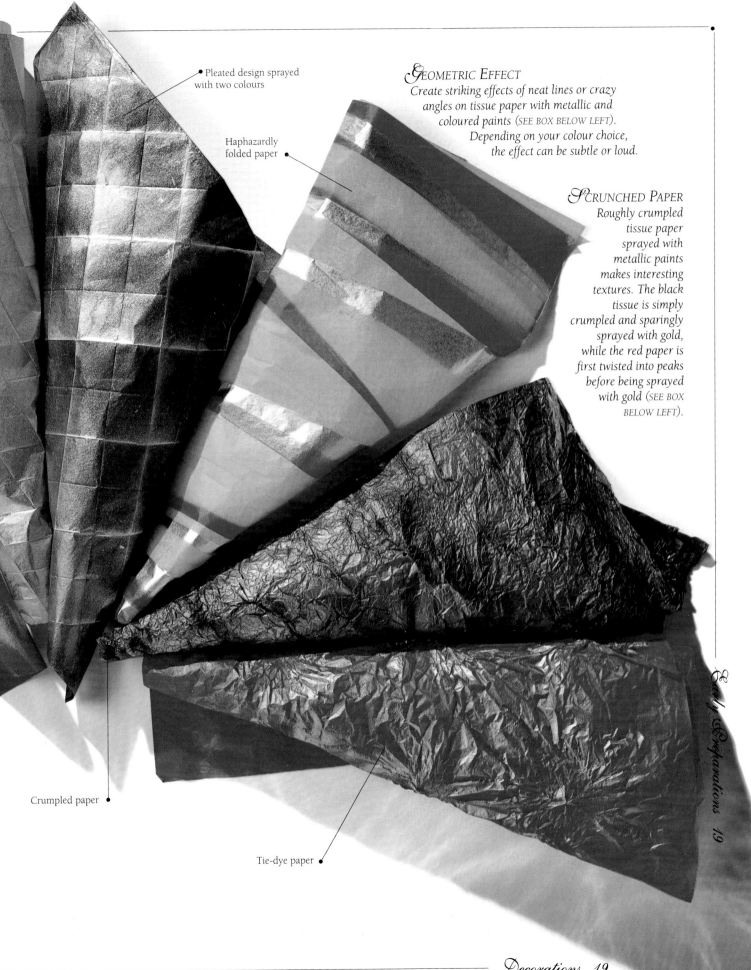

Pleated design sprayed
with two colours

Haphazardly
folded paper

Crumpled paper

Tie-dye paper

GEOMETRIC EFFECT
Create striking effects of neat lines or crazy
angles on tissue paper with metallic and
coloured paints (SEE BOX BELOW LEFT).
Depending on your colour choice,
the effect can be subtle or loud.

SCRUNCHED PAPER
Roughly crumpled
tissue paper
sprayed with
metallic paints
makes interesting
textures. The black
tissue is simply
crumpled and sparingly
sprayed with gold,
while the red paper is
first twisted into peaks
before being sprayed
with gold (SEE BOX
BELOW LEFT).

CHRISTMAS CHAINS

DECORATING THE HOME ADDS TO the excitement of Christmas. The Christmas tree always makes an impact, especially at night when its twinkling lights give the only light in the room. Flower arrangements also bring a room to life, creating both a visual focus and a delicious fragrance. Add to these decorations some original and colourful paper chains, and your rooms will be transformed – not, of course, by magic but by a certain amount of hard work.

It is fun making paper chains because everyone can join in. The garlands and chains shown here are easy to make and can be completed well in advance of Christmas.

STRING OF STARS
Make a chain of metallic green stars, using a template (SEE PAGE 116).

Gold cord

LORDS AND LADIES
The template for this chain (SEE PAGE 116) is cunningly designed to give you a row of alternating female and male figures. If the chain is going to be viewed from both sides, glue two sheets of paper to each other first. Use thin paper, as thick paper can be quite difficult to fold and cut.

Lords and Ladies

FLOWERED GARLAND
Cut twenty-two 10 cm (4 in) squares from tissue paper with pinking shears, and then pleat and crush to give them texture. Pull them straight and wrap each around a 1.2 m (4 ft) length of gold or silver cord. Tie one end tightly with reel wire. Turn the paper back so that the wire tie is inside, and covered by the tissue flower.

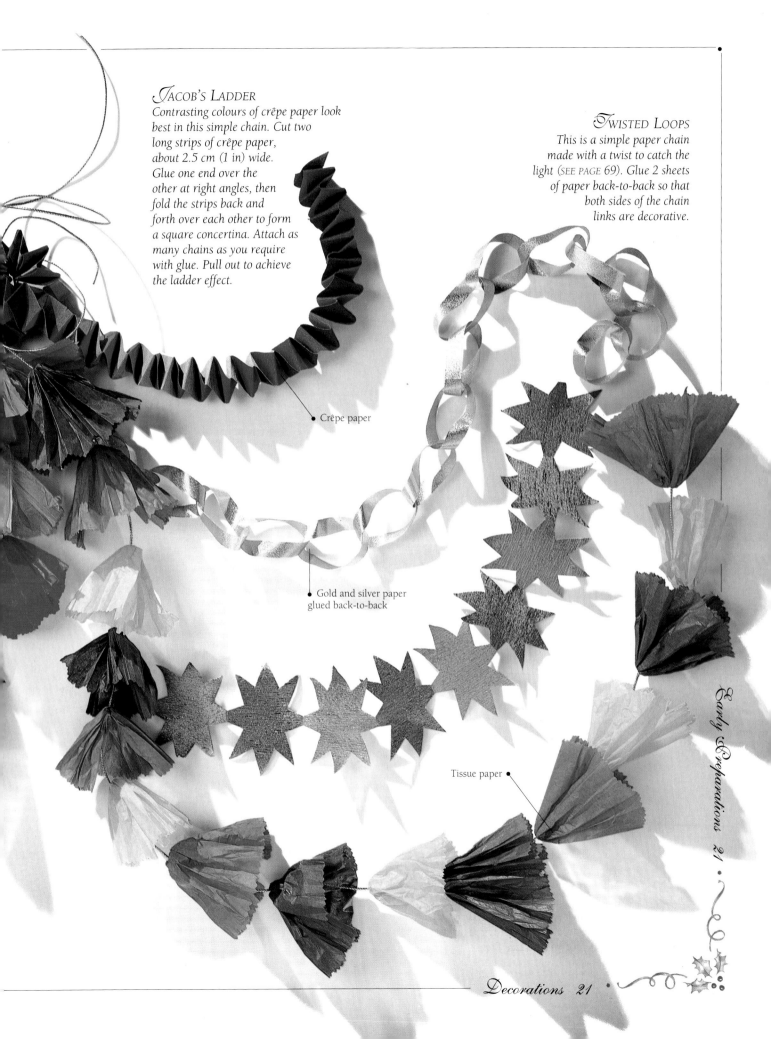

Jacob's Ladder

Contrasting colours of crêpe paper look best in this simple chain. Cut two long strips of crêpe paper, about 2.5 cm (1 in) wide. Glue one end over the other at right angles, then fold the strips back and forth over each other to form a square concertina. Attach as many chains as you require with glue. Pull out to achieve the ladder effect.

Twisted Loops

This is a simple paper chain made with a twist to catch the light (SEE PAGE 69). Glue 2 sheets of paper back-to-back so that both sides of the chain links are decorative.

Crêpe paper

Gold and silver paper glued back-to-back

Tissue paper

Exotic Paper Flowers

FLOWERS MADE FROM TISSUE PAPER, thin card, and crêpe paper, in colours that are as riotous or gentle as you like, look difficult to make but are actually quite simple. I've chosen bright colours for the large flowers, orange-peaches and apricots for the roses, and pastels for the bell flowers, colours that are in keeping with the shapes of the flowers.

Bell Flowers
These flowers look perfect in soft shades. Make them from coloured card and give them paper-ribbon stamens. Attach a loop of thin wire or thread to the stamens if you want to hang the flowers.

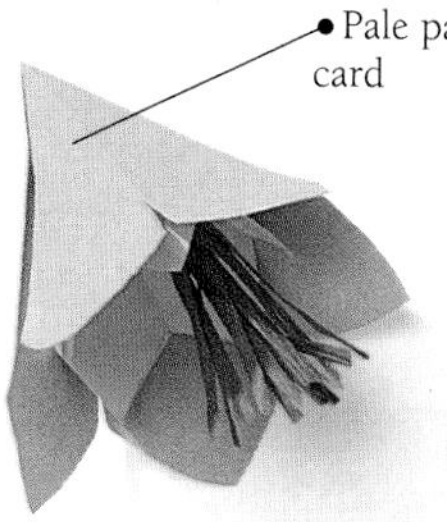

Pale pastel card

Paper-ribbon stamen

Jazzy Blooms
Choose brilliantly coloured tissue paper to make extravagant peonies, then set them off with a green ruff.

Vibrant tissue paper

Orange and apricot crêpe paper

What You Need
Mossing wire
Peonies
Three 51 x 38 cm (20 x 15 in) tissue paper
Bell Flowers
14 x 7.5 cm (5½ x 3 in) and 10 x 6.5 cm (4 x 2½ in) thin card
4 x 9 cm (1½ x 3½ in) paper ribbon
Paper glue
Roses
Ten 10 x 7.5 cm (4 x 3 in) crêpe paper

Peach and pink crêpe paper

• Pinked edge

Hot-pink, and red tissue paper

CREPE ROSES

Use the template to cut out
five inner and five outer petals for each crêpe rose
(SEE PAGE 116). Arrange them in a posy and secure the
narrow ends together with mossing wire. They look startling
and effective in brilliant colours, and even better in two
shades. Take your inspiration from real roses or take
them into the realms of fantasy wih strange colours,
such as grey and blue, or chocolate and lilac.

PAPER BELL FLOWERS & PEONIES

USE PAPER FLOWERS to adorn presents, or the
Christmas tree. They last well, so this year's tree
decorations can dress next year's gifts.

⁓⁄⁄ PAPER BELL FLOWERS ⁓⁄⁄

1 Use the templates from page
116 to make your own
templates for the petals, with
diameters of 7 cm
(2½ in) and 5 cm
(2 in), and a
7.5 cm (3 in)
stamen, cutting one
end into thin strips.

2 Fold the outer
petals along the
fold lines, gluing the
tab on the inside. Do
the same for the inner petals.

3 Put a drop of
glue on the
base of the inner
petals and stick it
into the outer flower. Roll the
uncut end of the paper ribbon and
glue it into the flower to finish.

⁓⁄⁄ TISSUE PAPER PEONY ⁓⁄⁄

1 Gather several pieces of coloured
tissue together into 1 cm (½ in) wide
pleats, then crumple and twist to form
narrow rolls. Uneven pleating and
crumpling is fine.

2 With pinking shears, cut
several 7.5 cm (3 in)
lengths from the rolls. Make
hanging loops from the wire.

3 Bind the ends of
several rolls with
wire, securing the
loop, and unruffle
the tissue to form the
petals of the flower.

FOREST STILL LIFE

TWIGS, PINE CONES, PAPER RIBBON, moss, and sprigs of fir combine in an inexpensive arrangement that is fun to create. It is easy to put together and, unlike fresh-flower arrangements, will not die in a few days. Woodland plant material makes lovely arrangements. Bark, twigs, boughs, pine cones, and foliage all have strong shapes and, because they all grow together naturally, look absolutely right when combined in the home. The paper ribbon in this creation is rough enough to join the "woodsy crew" – a more refined silk ribbon would have been out of place. Dried arrangements look especially effective displayed in glass containers. You may, at first, assume that the shiny quality of glass would seem at odds with rugged plant material. If you line the vase with moss, wood, bark, leaves, petals, dried mushrooms, or ginger roots, however, the overall effect is spectacular, and you end up with a container that enhances, rather than detracts from, the arrangement.

Orange-red paper ribbon

WHAT YOU NEED
Two 23 x 11 x 8 cm (9 x 4½ x 3 in) dry foam blocks
Adhesive clay
Florists' spikes
Blunt knife
3 large handfuls red-dyed lichen
35 woodland twigs, 25 cm (10 in) long
20 cm- (8 in-) square glass container
3.5 m (11 ft) paper ribbon
6 giant pine cones
Glue
Stub wires
7 sprigs blue fir

METHOD
Cut blocks of dry foam to fit inside the container, leaving a 2 cm (¾ in) gap at the sides. Secure them in place with adhesive clay and florists' spikes. Using a blunt knife, wedge clumps of lichen and a few twigs down the sides of the container to hide the foam. With unfurled paper ribbon, firmly tie twigs together in twos and threes to make interesting shapes: some at angles to each other, and others running parallel. Leave the ribbon ends long. Build up an interesting form, like this tower, and crown with a pine cone glued in position. Wire in more cones and then dress the arrangement with blue fir. Splay out the ribbon ends (and cut some back) to finish the arrangement with a flourish.

ℐNSTANT IMPACT
With its dramatic, angular outline,
and the vibrant, contrasting colours
found in the ribbons and foliage,
this dried arrangement has
tremendous visual impact.

• Giant, pine cone

• Woodland twigs
attached with
paper ribbon

HAND-PAINTED CANDLE
I have decorated this apricot
candle with poster paints,
which match the colours of
the arrangement. Water
down the paints to the right
colour and then mix with a
couple of drops of washing-up
liquid – this makes the paint
adhere to the candle.
Paint freehand or
use stencils
to achieve
beautiful
designs.

Blue fir •

• Red-dyed lichen

Square glass •
container

CORNUCOPIA

WALL HANGINGS have much to commend them. Because they sit flat against a wall, they take up little space, yet they can be striking, especially when made in an unusual shape. Think of these almost one-dimensional decorations as paintings that can take many forms – swags, columns, panels, cornucopias, baskets, or even hanging Christmas trees (SEE PAGES 60–61).

A cornucopia is such a symbol of overflowing richness: it just has to be filled to the brim with a profusion of colourful flowers and fruits. You can make your cornucopia, or indeed any of the other wall hangings, from both fresh and dried material. If you use fresh material, you will have to work shortly before the time your decoration is going on display, but if you use dried flowers, seeds, nuts, and fruit, you can complete the arrangement well in advance of Christmas. Store it in a dry place, ideally away from the light so that the colours do not fade.

WHAT YOU NEED

Two 71 x 46 cm (28 x 18 in)
chicken wire
Wire cutters
8 handfuls dried moss
Mossing wire
70 dried yarrow flowerheads
60 dried red roses
14 dried pink larkspur
12 dried hydrangeas
10 dried Nigella orientalis
seedheads
Stub wires
7 gilded pomegranates
1 m (3 ft) paper ribbon
Picture hook

METHOD

Cut the 2 pieces of chicken wire into a horn shape. Tightly sandwich a 1.5 cm (½ in) layer of moss between the pieces of chicken wire and sew the edges together with mossing wire. Keep the moss in place by looping pieces of wire through the frame and tying firmly. Either stick the flowers and seedheads directly into the moss, or wire their stems with stub wire first, then poke into the base. If using lightweight flowers, glue them in position. Push a stub wire into each pomegranate, through the newspaper stuffing, then wire into position. Make single bows from the paper ribbon (SEE PAGES 96–97) and wire into the arrangement. Wall hangings are surprisingly light: a picture hook holds them in place.

• Red rose

Yarrow flowerhead •

GILDED POMEGRANATES

Enhance the form and colour of pomegranates with gold paint and sugar.

1 *Cut a 4 cm (1½ in) hole in the base of the pomegranate and scoop the seeds out with a spoon. Fill the pomegranate with newspaper or dry foam to absorb moisture. Leave in a warm place to dry.*

2 *When dried, spray the top of the pomegranate with gold paint. Lightly sprinkle sugar over the wet paint so it adheres.*

Gilded
pomegranate

Pink larkspur

Nigella
orientalis
seedhead

Salmon-pink,
paper ribbon

Hydrangea

YEAR-ROUND COLOUR
*This rich, sunny-coloured cornucopia
of flowers and fruit looks pretty hanging
on a wall at any time of year. As the
seasons pass, change the varieties of fruit
and flowers spilling out of it.*

POMEGRANATE & PEONY WREATH

THE BEAUTY OF MAKING WREATHS and circlets with dried flowers is that you can prepare them ahead of time and at your leisure. If they do not look too "Christmassy", you can use them to decorate a door or wall for many months. Air-dried larkspur, small-flowered hybrid tea roses, peonies, helichrysum, and yarrow, as well as most silica-dried flowers, all keep their colours well, so long as they are not put in a sunny or very bright position in a room. I particularly enjoy mixing reds and pinks together; they always make an arrangement look so lively. Adding greenery keeps the flowers looking new and sparkling. I like to use preserved ivy, commonly available from florists' shops. Steeped in glycerine and dye, the leaves appear fresh and keep their strong colour indefinitely.

*TWIG CIRCLET
A twig circlet decorated with preserved ivy leaves, dried, bright yellow helichrysum, dried red roses, rust- and gold-painted pine cones, and crab apples.*

PRESERVED FLOWERS

MANY-PETALLED FLOWERS that are unsuitable for air-drying can be preserved in silica crystals.

1 *Half fill a container that you can seal with silica crystals. Push a stub wire into the base of the flower and place on the silica.*

2 *Carefully spoon silica crystals over and between the petals, covering the flower completely. Seal the container. The flower will have dried in 2 days.*

WHAT YOU NEED
*Green binding tape
31 cm- (12 in-) diameter foam circle
5 gilded pomegranates
(SEE PAGE 26)
Glue gun
5 handfuls dried moss
Dark green spray paint
1.2 m (4 ft) fabric tubing stuffed with cotton wool
7 wired, glycerined and dyed hydrangas
2 wired, dried peonies
10 wired sprays dried, pink roses
8 wired sprays dried, red roses
20 wired sprigs glycerined and dyed ivy
Fabric hanging loop*

METHOD
Wrap the green binding tape around the foam circle. Indent the foam where you want to place the pomegranates, then glue into position, using a glue gun. Spray-paint the moss dark green. When dry, glue the moss to the wreath to provide a natural-looking base. Wind the fabric tubing around the wreath, then tie secure. Wire in the larger flowers, and then insert the smaller ones in curves against the fabric. Next, wire in the ivy. Attach the fabric loop to the top and back of the wreath for hanging.

Glycerined and dyed
hydrangea

FRUITS AND FLOWERS

*Gilded and sugared pomegranates nestle
among sprigs of ivy, dried flowers, and
striped fabric. The vibrantly coloured
peonies and roses compete for space
with the pomegranates, creating
an effect of overflowing richness.*

Peony

Gilded
pomegranate

Spray of
pink roses

Striped fabric

Glycerined and
dyed ivy leaf

Spray of red roses

Early Preparations 30

Bread Wreaths

THEY SAY BREAD never falls but on its buttered side. Well, these wondrously decorative breads need never see a speck of butter. Made to hang on the wall, they last for years, or at least until dust gets the better of them. Decorative but inedible breads, made from a simple flour, salt, and water recipe, are very popular in Scandinavia. You can make them into a variety of shapes, as small decorations to hang on the Christmas tree, or larger wall hangings in the forms of baskets, hearts, wreaths, and houses. Alternatively, prepare a decorative yeast bread for eating – what you gain on texture and flavour, you lose in the fine definition of the shapes, however.

Raffia hanging rope

Whole cloves

Salt dough basket

SALT DOUGH
340 g (12 oz) plain flour
270 g (9½ oz) salt
4–5 drops cooking oil
Onion skin and cloves to decorate
Beaten egg white to glaze

Mix the flour, salt, and oil; add water to form a stiff dough. Knead until smooth. Form a base for the basket. Roll out a third of the dough to a 6 mm (¼ in) thickness. Cut out a basket shape (keep remaining dough covered). Place on a baking tray covered with greaseproof paper. Shape remaining dough into flowers, fruits, and strips for the basket weave and handle. Attach to the base with water. Decorate. Glaze with egg white. Bake at 110° C (225° F) for 8 hours, until it is golden and completely dried out.

HANGING BASKETS
You can make a glazed bread basket of fruits and flowers from either salt dough, which will last for years, or from yeast dough, which can be admired both for its looks and its delicious taste.

PLAIN WHITE BREAD
1 tbs active dried yeast
475 ml (16 fl oz) lukewarm water
680 g (1½ lb) strong white flour
1 tbs salt
Onion skin to decorate
Beaten egg yolk to glaze

Sprinkle the yeast over 4 tablespoons of the lukewarm water. Mix the flour and salt in a large bowl. Pour the dissolved yeast and the rest of the water into the flour and salt, and mix to form a stiff dough. Knead until smooth. Let rise for 1–1½ hours. Punch down. Shape as for the salt dough recipe, bearing in mind that when the dough rises the appearance will alter slightly. Insert a leather thong for hanging. Place on a baking tray covered with grease-proof paper. Let rise for 15 minutes. Glaze with egg yolk. Bake at 180º C (350º F) for 35–45 minutes, until it is a rich, golden brown.

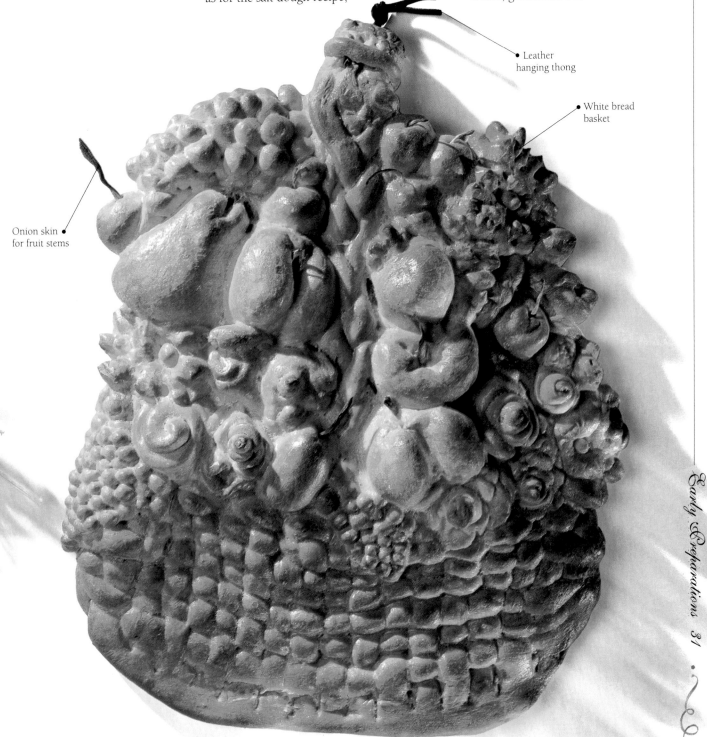

Leather hanging thong

White bread basket

Onion skin for fruit stems

SPICE WREATH

MAKE A WREATH THAT IS both fragrant and beautiful. A base of pine, deliciously scented in itself, can last for many months. (Good quality, plastic, pine garlanding can be incredibly realistic, and will last forever, although you have to forgo the fragrance.) Decorate the base with citrus pomanders, little bags made from paper ribbon and filled with crushed spices, and small bundles of lavender and cinnamon sticks. All have such strong scents that the wreath will continue to perfume the air long after the festive season has passed.

WHAT YOU NEED
152 x 15 cm (60 x 6 in)
chicken wire
10 handfuls dry moss
20 wired evergreens
Mossing wire
Stub wires
Three 6 cm- (2½ in-) diameter
terracotta pots
7 paper-ribbon spice bags
3 lavender bundles
3 cinnamon-stick bundles
7 citrus pomanders
16 sprigs dried hops
Glue
4 decorative seedheads
2 bunches eucalyptus seedheads
7 pine cones
3 sprigs marjoram
3 m (10 ft) paper ribbon

METHOD
Make a moss-filled chicken-wire frame (SEE PAGE 57), inserting wired evergreens to cover, and bend it into a heart shape. Attach stub wires to the pots, spice bags, lavender and cinnamon-stick bundles, and pomanders, and secure to the wreath. Fill pots with hops. Glue on seedheads, pine cones, and marjoram. Hang with a paper-ribbon bow.

BUNCH OF HOPS
Tie dried hops and cinnamon sticks together with mossing wire, cover with a matching bow, and glue on eucalyptus seedheads to make a simple, scented bunch. Pick and air-dry hops just as they form the seedheads. If you wait any longer, the seedheads easily shatter.

• Pink, paper ribbon

Cinnamon stick

• Dried hops

CITRUS POMANDERS

THESE POMANDERS CONTINUE to release their sharp, clovey scent for many years.

1 Pierce holes all over the surface of a lime, or other small citrus fruit, with a skewer. Insert a whole clove into each hole.

2 Put ground orris root in a paper bag. Place the lime in the bag, seal, and shake to cover with ground orris root. Store in a warm, dark place for 3 weeks. Remove from the bag and display with a raffia tie.

Paper-ribbon bow

Dried hops

Decorative seedhead

Marjoram

Bag of spices

Eucalyptus seedhead

Lavender bundle

Lime pomander

Spicy Heart
This fragrant wreath
looks perfect hanging in a
kitchen and also in a hallway,
where its rich scents will be
fully appreciated.

Cinnamon-stick bundle

Advent Wreath

THE WORD "ADVENT" means an arrival or coming, especially one that is awaited. This event in the Christian year is marked by the four Sundays that precede Christ's birth. In many countries, Advent is celebrated in the home as well as in church with an Advent wreath of evergreen foliage holding five candles. Each Sunday in Advent you light a candle – the fifth and final one is lit on Christmas Day. Traditionally, the candles for the four Sundays are red, although the third candle may be pink to match the minister's vestments during that week. The Christmas Day candle is white.

To draw attention to the candles, make the wreath with rich, green foliage. Several conifers last amazingly well indoors, keeping both their colour and their needles, and White fir and Colorado spruce are both excellent. Over the evergreen base, add some dried flowers in reds, silver lichen, moss, pine cones, and ribbon.

The Advent wreath looks best on a table, with the white candle placed in the centre. For safety, always stay nearby while the candles are lit, and do not allow them to burn too low.

Silver lichen

White fir

Pine cone

Monterey cypress

What You Need

152 x 15 cm (5 ft x 6 in)
 chicken wire
15 handfuls damp moss
38 x 15 cm (15 x 6 in)
 chicken wire
Mossing wire
Wire cutters
10 sprigs White fir
10 sprigs Monterey cypress
10 dried Celosia
15 dried Helichrysum
18 small pieces dried
 silver lichen
12 small, pine cones
1 m (3 ft) gold-edged,
 green ribbon
4, thick, red candles
1, thick, white candle

Method

Make a moss-filled chicken-wire frame (SEE PAGE 57) and bend it into a square. With the smaller piece of chicken wire, make a moss-filled tube and place it diagonally across the square, wiring it in at the corners. Cut an 8 cm (3 in) slit through the frame in each corner and in the centre and pull apart to make holes to hold the candles. Insert the foliage into the frame to cover, and decorate with the dried flowers, lichen, pine cones, and ribbon. Finally, add the candles.

Gold-edged, green ribbon

Thick, columnar candle

CHRISTMAS HERALD

Place this simple Advent wreath on a table beside a window, to enjoy it from outdoors as well as indoors. If you use long-lasting foliage, lichen, and dried flowers, in rich shades of reds, this wreath still looks its best on Christmas Day, when you light the final, white candle.

Helichrysum

Celosia

Miss Jeffers's Cake

It would seem paradoxical that a rich Christmas cake should feature in the quirky cuisine of tropical Nevis in the West Indies. Miss Jeffers, though, would make this irresistible cake for us when we were staying on the island. The decorations are my addition.

Ingredients
1.5 kg (3 lb) raisins
680 g (1½ lb) currants
455 g (1 lb) prunes
170 g (6 oz) cocktail cherries
340 g (12 oz) candied peel
1½ tsp each ground cinnamon,
   cloves, nutmeg, and salt
240 ml (8 fl oz) brandy
120 ml (4 fl oz) rum
2 tbs Madeira
4 tsp vanilla essence
115 g (4 oz) each chopped
   almonds and Brazil nuts
680 g (1½ lb) demerara sugar
680 g (1½ lb) butter
14 eggs (size 2)
680 g (1½ lb) plain flour
Juice and rind of 8 limes

Method
Mix the fruit, peel, and spices in a large bowl. Sprinkle with the alcohol and vanilla essence, cover, and leave for 2 days. Toast the nuts, and set aside. In a large bowl, beat the sugar and butter until light and fluffy. In another bowl, lightly beat the eggs. Slowly beat the eggs into the butter and sugar. Stir in the flour. Stir in the steeped fruit, lime juice and rind, and nuts. Transfer the mixture into a greased and lined 31 cm (12in) square baking tin. Bake for 7 hours at 140° C (275° F). Store in a sealed tin until ready to decorate just before Christmas.

Leafy Ruff
I always decorate this cake with a ruff of holly and pine (left). In Nevis, Miss Jeffers uses tropical flowers on her cakes.

- Sugared, rose petal
- Sugared, white grape
- Toasted almond
- Apricot-stuffed prune
- Crystallized ginger
- Toasted pecan
- Toasted Brazil nut
- Sugared kumquat
- Marzipan-stuffed prune
- Crystallized fig
- Crystallized orange peel
- Crystallized cranberry in sliced angelica

FLOWERS, FRUIT, & NUTS

ONE WEEK BEFORE CHRISTMAS, brush this delicious cake with melted apricot jam, and arrange the tantalizing decorations on top.

⁄⁄⁄ APRICOT-STUFFED PRUNES ⁄⁄⁄

1 With a small, sharp knife, carefully remove the stones from each of the prunes, keeping the fruit as neat and intact as possible.

2 Between your fingers and the work surface, roll small amounts of cooled, thick apricot purée (made from dried apricots, water, and sugar) into almond-shaped pieces that will fit into the holes in the prunes.

3 Stuff each prune with an apricot piece. You can also stuff the prunes with marzipan instead of apricot purée.

⁄⁄⁄ SUGARED ROSE PETALS ⁄⁄⁄

1 Gently pull the petals free from 1 scented, well-formed rose with a good colour.

2 With a small paintbrush, lightly coat each rose petal all over with lightly beaten egg white, taking care not to saturate it.

3 Sift caster sugar through a sieve over the rose petals, turning them carefully to cover all sides. Leave them to dry in a warm place on greaseproof paper for several hours.

4 Re-create the rose, using a piece of crystallized ginger as the centrepiece.

CRYSTALLIZED FRUIT

HOMEMADE CRYSTALLIZED FRUITS are one of those traditional Christmas delicacies that are just too good to be passed over in favour of shop-bought ones. Although the two-week preparation seems long-winded, the amount of time involved each day is small, and the results are absolutely scrumptious. The homemade versions have much more flavour than shop-bought ones, which I have always found too sweet, and as they last for months in a sealed container, they can be made well ahead of the Christmas rush.

Experiment with all kinds of fruit. Citrus fruits are particularly good. So, too, are tasty plums, apricots, and cherries. Ginger, however, is my all-time favourite, and it also makes an excellent *digestif* after rich food. Crystallized figs and pineapple tend to be rather sweet, but cranberries retain a tang that I find irresistible.

Fig

Prune

Lemon slice

Pink grapefruit segments

Ginger

Whole clementine

Carlsbad plum

INGREDIENTS
*450 g (1 1b) fruit (such as
    citrus fruits, plums, apricots,
    cherries, figs, pineapple,
    cranberries) or cut ginger
    root, peeled*
300 ml (½ pt) water
675 g (1½ lb) granulated sugar

METHOD
Simmer the fruit or ginger root in the water in a heavy saucepan, until blanched but still firm. Remove the fruit with a slotted spoon and place in a baking dish. Dissolve 175 g (6 oz) of the sugar in the poaching water. Pour the syrup over the fruit, cover, and leave for 24 hours. On the second day, drain the syrup from the fruit into a saucepan, add 50 g (2 oz) sugar, and heat until it dissolves. Pour over the fruit, cover, and leave for 24 hours. Repeat each day, until Day 8. On Day 8, dissolve 75 g (3 oz) sugar in the syrup, pour over the fruit, cover, and leave for 2 days. On Day 10, dissolve 75 g (3 oz) sugar in the syrup, pour over the fruit, cover, and leave for 4 days. On Day 14, place fruit on a rack, with greaseproof paper underneath, and leave to dry in a warm place.

Cranberry

Miniature
pineapple
slices

Sweet, Sticky Spiral

A luscious spiral of sweet and
tangy crystallized fruits with a
dusting of granulated sugar. The
sharpest flavours come from the citrus
fruits, particularly the segments of pink
grapefruit. Cherries and cranberries also
retain their strong flavours, as do the small
chunks of ginger. Pineapple, figs, and plums tend
toward the sweeter end of the flavour spectrum.

Cherry

LIQUEUR FRUITS

AT CHRISTMAS, AS A CHILD, I was wickedly treated to a prune or two that had been preserved in Armagnac. I adored them then, and still do now. What is so wonderful about liqueur fruits is that the alcohol lends its tantalizing flavour to the fruit and, in turn, the fruit flavours the alcohol, so that each tastes just delicious, yet different from the other. Most ripe, perfect fruits can be preserved in rubber-sealed jars solely in alcohol that is 25 per cent proof or higher, or in a mixture of syrup and alcohol. Liqueur fruits should be allowed to mature for at least six weeks, and they keep for years. Serve small portions of fruit with some of the liqueur as an after-dinner drink, or try it poured over ice cream.

Muscat Raisins in Liqueur

Kumquats & Limequats in Rum

Blackberries in Kirsch

BLACKBERRIES IN KIRSCH
680 g (1½ lb) firm, ripe blackberries
230 g (8 oz) redcurrants
230 g (8 oz) caster sugar
Redcurrant leaves, optional
445 ml (¾ pt) kirsch

Layer the fruit and sugar in three 500-ml (1-pt) jars, leaving 1 cm (½ in) headroom. Decorate with redcurrant leaves pushed between the fruit and the glass, if you wish. Pour kirsch over the fruit to cover completely. Tightly seal and leave in a cool, dark place for at least 6 weeks.

KUMQUATS & LIMEQUATS IN RUM
890 ml (1½ pt) water
230 g (8 oz) caster sugar
455 g (1 lb) kumquats, pricked
230 g (8 oz) limequats, pricked
1.8 litre (3 pt) white rum

Bring the water and sugar to the boil, and simmer until the sugar dissolves. Add the fruit and simmer for 5 minutes. Place in two 1-litre (1½-pt) jars, leaving 1 cm (½ in) headroom. Reduce the syrup to 295 ml (½ pt). Remove from the heat and add the rum. Pour over the fruit. Tightly seal and leave in a cool, dark place for 4 weeks.

MUSCAT RAISINS IN LIQUEUR
455 g (1 lb) muscat raisins
890 ml (1½ pt) strong Earl Grey tea
740 ml (1¼ pt) muscat liqueur

Soak the raisins in the tea overnight. Drain the raisins, and discard the tea. Place the raisins in a 1-litre (2-pt) jar, leaving 1 cm (½ in) headroom. Cover them with muscat liqueur. Seal tightly and leave in a cool, dark place for 8 weeks, shaking the jar gently, about once a week.

Mixed Fruits in Brandy

PRUNES & APPLES IN ARMAGNAC
1 kg (2 lb) best quality prunes
230 g (8 oz) dried apple rings
1.5 litre (2½ pt) apple juice
445 ml (¾ pt) Armagnac

Place the prunes, apple rings, and apple juice in a saucepan. Bring to the boil, then remove the saucepan from the heat and leave the fruit to soak overnight. Remove the fruit, discarding the juice, and arrange in two 1-litre (1½-pt) jars, leaving 1 cm (½ in) headroom. Pour the Armagnac over the fruit to cover completely. Tightly seal the jars and leave in a cool, dark place for at least 6 weeks.

PEARS & CHERRIES IN PORT
740 ml (1¼ pt) port
455 g (1 lb) caster sugar
½ cinnamon stick
5 cloves
1.5 kg (3 lb) firm pears
455 g (1 lb) cherries

Bring the port, sugar, and spices to the boil, and stir until the sugar dissolves. Add the fruit and simmer for 20 minutes. Place the fruit in a 2.5-litre (5.3-pt) jar, leaving 1 cm (½ in) headroom. Boil the remaining syrup until it has reduced to 445 ml (¾ pt). Strain, then pour over the fruit to cover. Close. Place the jar in a roasting pan filled with water in a 150° C (325° F) oven for 1 hour to seal. Leave in a cool, dark place for at least 6 weeks.

Prunes & Apples in Armagnac

Pears & Cherries in Port

MIXED FRUITS IN BRANDY
5 small, white peaches
455 g (1 lb) apricots
4 tamarillos, sliced
1 miniature pineapple, sliced
  (with peel left on)
3 kiwi fruit, peeled and sliced
10 tangerines, peeled
4 star fruit, sliced
890 ml (1½ pt) water
455 g (1 lb) caster sugar
Juice of 4 limes
2 vanilla pods
740 ml (1¼ pt) brandy

Blanch the fruit in boiling water, and remove the peach and apricot skins. Bring the measured water, sugar, lime juice, and vanilla pods to the boil. When the sugar has dissolved, add the fruit, and poach for 6 minutes. Layer the fruit in a 6-litre (1½-gallon) glass jar, leaving 1 cm (½ in) headroom. Add the brandy to the syrup and pour over the fruit to cover. Close. Place the jar in a roasting pan filled with water in a 150° C (325° F) oven for 1 hour to seal. Leave in a cool, dark place for at least 6 weeks.

TRIO OF PUDDINGS

THE TRADITIONAL Christmas pudding is utterly delicious, but many find it far too rich at the end of Christmas dinner. If you love the flavours of Christmas pudding, but would prefer something a fraction lighter, try one of the two other puddings. If you find each one to your taste, make all three!

Ice Cream Pudding •

FROZEN FRUIT
All the flavours of the traditional pudding trapped in a light, frozen cream.

• Dried fruit

• White holly leaf

ICE CREAM PUDDING
115 g (4 oz) mixed dried fruit
30 g (1 oz) glacé cherries
30 g (1 oz) candied peel
4 tbs brandy
445 ml (¾ pt) double cream
85 g (3 oz) caster sugar
85 g (3 oz) fine, wholemeal breadcrumbs
½ tsp ground cinnamon
85 g (3 oz) brown sugar

Mix the fruit and candied peel in a bowl. Sprinkle it with brandy, cover, and leave overnight.

Chop the fruit and peel into small pieces. Beat the cream and sugar until thickened. Chill in the freezer until almost set, stirring every half hour.

Meanwhile, combine the breadcrumbs, cinnamon, and brown sugar, then place on a baking tray. Toast at 200° C (400° F) for 5–10 minutes, until golden and caramelized. Let cool, then break up into small pieces. Stir the soaked fruit and peel, and the caramel pieces into the cream mix. Freeze until it is solid. Remove 15 minutes before serving. Unmould carefully. Serves 8.

CHRISTMAS BOMBE
85 g (3 oz) mixed dried fruit
½ tsp ground cinnamon
½ tsp ground cloves
½ tsp ground nutmeg
5 tbs rum
3 eggs and 2 egg yolks (size 2)
60 g (2 oz) caster sugar
295 ml (½ pt) double cream
15 g (½ oz) gelatin
38 cm (15 in) sponge roll

Mix the dried fruit and spices in a bowl. Sprinkle with 2 tbs of the rum, cover, and leave overnight.

Beat the eggs and egg yolks for 5 minutes, until foamy. Continue whisking, and slowly add the sugar.

Beat for 5 more minutes. Stir in the soaked fruit. Lightly whip the cream, and then fold into the fruit mixture. Heat the rest of the rum just below boiling. Sprinkle the gelatin over the rum; stir until dissolved. Stir the melted gelatin into the fruit mixture. Line a 19 x 9 cm (7½ x 3½ in) basin with 5 mm (¼ in) sponge roll slices. Spoon the fruit mixture into the mould. Cover with the remaining slices of sponge roll. Cover and refrigerate the bombe for several hours before serving. Unmould carefully. Serves 10.

HIDDEN FLAVOUR
A Christmas bombe with
swirls of sponge hides the
lightest mousse, which
carries all of the flavours
of a Christmas pudding.

• Christmas
Bombe

ULTIMATE PUDDING
Luscious fruits, nuts, and spices and
a great deal of alcohol make this
the ultimate in rich Christmas
puddings. Use a round
mould for an old-
fashioned finish.

• Traditional
Christmas Pudding

• Variegated holly

TRADITIONAL CHRISTMAS PUDDING
230 g (8 oz) unsalted butter
2 tbs black treacle
180 ml (6 fl oz) brandy
Juice and grated rind of 2 lemons
Grated rind of 2 oranges
4 eggs (size 2)
230 g (8 oz) wholemeal breadcrumbs
230 g (8 oz) each currants, sultanas, and
    muscat raisins
230 g (8 oz) muscovado sugar
85 g (3 oz) wholemeal flour
85 g (3 oz) almonds, chopped and toasted
85 g (3 oz) hazelnuts, chopped and toasted
85 g (3 oz) crystallized ginger, chopped
1 large cooking apple, chopped
1 tsp each ground allspice and nutmeg
½ tsp ground cloves

Melt the butter and treacle
in a saucepan over a low
heat. When cool, add the
brandy, lemon juice, and
lemon and orange rind,
then beat in the eggs. Mix
the remaining ingredients
in a large bowl. Stir the
egg mixture into the dry
ingredients. Place in a
well-greased 1 kg (2¼ lb)
round, pudding mould, and
steam for 6 hours. Cool for
10 minutes, then remove the
mould. Cover the Christmas
pudding in plastic wrap, and
store for 2 months. Steam
in the mould for a further
1½ hours before serving.
Serves 16.

Early Preparations 44

FLOWER & FOLIAGE ICE BOWL

THE INCREDIBLE BEAUTY OF FLOWERS, fruits, berries, and leaves trapped in translucent ice makes an ice bowl one of the most arresting, yet practical Christmas decorations. Serve ice creams, sorbets, fruit salads, or an ice-cold punch in it – anything that will benefit from the chilling effects of this unusual bowl.

Choose non-poisonous plant material that will fit into the 2 cm (¾ in) of ice that form the bowl. Berries look particularly good and, because the bowl can be made well ahead of Christmas, you can take advantage of the autumn crop of rowan, cotoneaster, and guelder rose fruits. Roses, freesias, lily petals, ferns, geranium leaves, herbs, and even the humble cabbage can be pressed into use. Slices of limes, tangerines, and kiwi and star fruits also look stunning.

WHAT YOU NEED
8.5 cm- (3¼ in-) tall jam jar
16 x 9 cm (6½ x 3½ in)
glass bowl
Matching 21 x 11 cm
(8½ x 4½ in) glass bowl
Clear tape
Non-poisonous plant material
Stub wire

Fern frond •

Honeysuckle •

• Mallow

• Cranesbill

FLORAL BOWL
Bring the summer garden to the
Christmas table with an ice bowl of flowers.
The pastel colours of honeysuckle, mallow, aster,
loosestrife, cranesbill, and fern make an enchanting
combination. If you plan to serve drinks from the
bowl, freeze small flowers in ice cubes.

FROZEN COLOUR
The glowing colours of the roses and berries, and the veining of the cabbage's leaves, look luscious suspended in ice. Fill the bowl with kir, a Champagne sorbet, or an exotic fruit salad.

• Loosestrife

Aster •

DECORATIVE ICE BOWLS

IF YOU ARE MAKING AN ICE BOWL for the first time, use fairly bulky plant material, such as roses and large leaves. You can easily wedge these in position. Small flowers tend to float to the top, so if you have chosen them, it is best to make the bowl in several stages, freezing thinner layers.

1 *Stack the jar and the bowls. Pour water between the 2 bowls until the water comes to 1 cm (½ in) below the rims. Fill the jar with water to keep the rims level. Hold in place with tape.*

2 *Select plant material for decorating the ice bowl. Here, I have chosen rowan berries, decorative cabbage leaves, miniature amaryllis flowers, sprigs of cypress, and small, red roses.*

3 *Slip the leaves and flowers into the water between the 2 bowls, prodding them into place with a stub wire. Wedge the larger leaves toward the bases of the bowls, and gently squeeze the flowers between the sides. Freeze overnight.*

4 *Remove the tape and jar, and pour cold water into the smaller bowl. Dip the outer bowl into cold water. (Warm water will cause the ice to crack.) The bowls will gradually come away from the ice. Place on a plate.*

Chapter Two

COUNTDOWN
TO CHRISTMAS

THE CHRISTMAS SEASON always arrives about two
weeks too early for me. The school holidays begin
at the same time, however, so you can rely on help
from children. Now is the time to make evergreen
arrangements, and decorate the Christmas tree.
Parties abound at this stage, calling for lavish
decorations and sumptuous food. Indulge in
wickedly rich food without feeling too guilty:
cream truffles, incredible jellies, and petits fours
all look breathtaking for special occasions.

EVERGREEN ENSEMBLE
*Make a long-lasting arrangement in a weathered
watering can. The rust hues of the mahonia echo the
colour of the pepper berries while golden dogwood
offsets the tufty pine, gold-striped elaeagnus, and
catkin sprays of garrya. Trails of small, green dates
and privet berries complete the arrangement.*

EVERGREEN WREATHS

THE SIMPLE FRONT DOOR WREATH made from evergreen foliage, twigs, and berries is a most evocative Christmas emblem, dating back to the pagan winter solstice festival. Brilliant red holly berries and rich green, winter leaves combine vibrantly, signalling the onslaught of cold weather in northern climes. In the past, whole branches of evergreen were hung above the front door. I have arranged foliage in a fan shape to make a change from the traditional wreath.

WOODLAND THEME
This evergreen wreath looks best unadorned, so that the natural beauty of the foliage commands all attention. It is most effective on both a simple, rustic front door and a more formal one.

Lichen-covered twig

Skimmia

WHAT YOU NEED
152 x 15 cm (60 x 6 in) chicken wire
10 handfuls damp moss
60 sprigs wired, berried skimmia
50 lichen-covered twigs
50 stems berried holly, leaves removed
Mossing wire

METHOD
Prepare a moss-filled chicken-wire frame (SEE PAGE 57), wiring skimmia sprigs into the front of the frame. Next, stick lichen-covered twigs and short pieces of holly into the frame, keeping them flowing in the same direction as the skimmia. Allow plant material to extend about 10 cm (4 in) beyond the frame's outer edge, but only 5–7.5 cm (2–3 in) over the inner edge. Wire the 2 ends of the wreath together.

Weatherproof,
red ribbon

Blue fir

*Extremely long-lasting, this hanging
bunch of conifer and holly needs only
a minimum of added decoration, in the
form of simple red bows. Its strong
shape is particularly suited to a
large, front door.*

Berried holly
with leaves removed

WHAT YOU NEED

*3 large, blue fir branches
5 stems berried holly,
leaves removed
3 small, blue fir branches
Mossing wire
4 m (12 ft) weatherproof,
red ribbon*

METHOD

Lay the large fir branches in
a fan shape on a flat surface. Overlap the cut
ends by about 5 cm (2 in). Arrange the holly on
top. Fill in any gaps with the smaller pieces of fir.
Tie the bunch firmly together with mossing wire.
Attach a hanging loop of wire or ribbon to the
back at the top. Cover with a bow and tie small
bows (SEE PAGES 96–97) among the branches.

WREATHS FROM HEAVEN

I FIND THE FRONT DOOR WREATH the most welcoming of all Christmas arrangements. Simple yet strong colour themes work best, for either minimal, evergreen wreaths made from holly, pine, and fir, or "over-the-top" glittery creations, like these vibrant gold and silver designs.

When making door wreaths, remember that they must be strong enough to withstand the rain and wind for about three weeks, not to mention the constant opening and closing of the front door. To keep the foliage fresh, stuff the chicken wire with damp moss. This makes a strong base for attaching both the foliage and any decorations.

GLOWING GOLD
Cherubs reach to catch the stars in this extravagant gold arrangement. The ribbon spiralling around the wreath echoes the curved shapes of the cherubs, creating a sparkling and lively decoration for your front door.

Golden, glittered lotus seedhead

Silvered star

Silvered cherub

Variegated holly

Miniature, wrapped parcel

Gilt Brazil nut

SILVER VARIATION
The same cherubs and stars, this time sprayed and glittered with silver, give the wreath a frosty look. Variegated holly and miniature, wrapped parcels add colour to the bottom half, and touches of red from the berries and ribbons introduce spots of warmth here and there.

WHAT YOU NEED
152 x 15 cm (60 x 6 in) chicken wire
10 handfuls damp moss
20 sprigs wired, long-lasting conifer
Mossing wire
Glue gun
Stub wires
2 cherubs and 3 stars, sprayed gold
7 Brazil nuts, sprayed gold
6 lotus seedheads, sprayed gold and glittered
7 brass baubles
2 m (6½ ft) gold, cellophane ribbon

METHOD
Make a circular, moss-filled chicken-wire frame (SEE PAGE 57), sticking wired sprigs of conifer into the frame to cover. Glue stub wires to the backs of the cherubs and stars, then stick them into the frame. Wire the nuts (SEE PAGE 61), seedheads, and baubles in position. Finally, twist gold, cellophane ribbon around the wreath, and make matching bows (SEE PAGES 96–97) and attach.

Gilt star

Gold,
cellophane
ribbon

Douglas fir

Brass
bauble

Gilt cherub

FLAMBOYANT FLOWERS

A LARGE FLOWER ARRANGEMENT has greater impact than a number of small ones. Give a large vase pride of place, and then arrange tiny vases with just a few of the flowers used in the main display around the rest of the house. Choose flowers with strong shapes that look good in silhouette, and stems and foliage with interesting forms. Here, cyclamen grow in their own pots, alongside cut holly, lilies, euphorbia, ranunculus, roses, strelitzia, and powerfully shaped gourds, with gold candles adding the dimension of light. They are all arranged in an antique copper.

Picotee cyclamen

Deep pink rose

WHAT YOU NEED
Large, oval, copper container
1 plastic bin liner
2 cyclamen plants
Two 23 x 11 x 8 cm (9 x 4½ x 3 in) dry foam blocks
Four 23 x 11 x 8 cm (9 x 4½ x 3 in) wet foam blocks, soaked
4 gold candles
7 stems Euphorbia fulgens
7 stems berried holly, leaves removed
7 roses
5 stems Euphorbia seguieriana
5 gloriosa lilies
5 ranunculus
5 strelitzia flowers
3 strelitzia leaves
3 gourds

Euphorbia seguieriana

METHOD
Line the container with the plastic bin liner, and position the plants. If necessary, raise them on dry foam. Fill the container with soaked wet foam, wedging it securely in place. Position the candles in the foam, adding more soaked wet foam for extra height, if necessary. Next, arrange the plant material so that it spills lavishly out of the container. Leave space around the candles, so that there is no risk of the display catching fire.

Gourd

Berried holly

Strelitzia leaf

GLOWING COLOUR
A weathered copper container
bursting with brash colour –
golden orange, military red,
and crushed pink – makes a
dramatic display for a hall
table or sideboard.

Euphorbia
fulgens

Strelitzia flower

Copper, a
dairy container

Gloriosa lily

BELL & ORB

HANG THESE EVERGREEN Christmas spheres in a porch or hallway, where they can be seen to best advantage throughout the festive season. If you use damp foam as a base, they will look fresh for at least two weeks, and even longer if you hang them outside. A traditional holly sphere is easy to make. The bell is only a little more complicated. I like to use berried holly by itself because it looks so rich. Mistletoe, however, looks rather sparse on its own, so I mix it with other foliage. Clementines add cheerful colour to arrangements, although you can use bright baubles instead.

Holly Bell
WHAT YOU NEED
30 x 18 x 18 cm (12 x 7 x 7 in) wet foam block, soaked
65 x 30 cm (26 x 12 in) chicken wire
Mossing wire
120 sprigs berried holly
4 m (13 ft) star-printed, green ribbon

• Variegated holly with berries

METHOD
Cut the foam to make a cone 30 cm (12 in) high, and 18 cm (7 in) wide at the base, tapering to 5 cm (2 in) at the top. Cover it with chicken wire, and secure with mossing wire. Tie several lengths of mossing wire to the top of the cone for extra strength and hang it at eye level, so you can work on it easily. Push short sprigs of berried holly into the top of the frame and long sprigs at the base, to accentuate the bell shape. Attach a bow at the top and base (SEE PAGES 96–97), and twist matching ribbon around the hanging wire.

• Gilt-edged green ribbon with gold stars

•Tangerine

•Mistletoe

Fruiting
ivy

Mistletoe Orb
WHAT YOU NEED
15 cm- (6 in-) square wet
foam block, soaked
50 x 30 cm (20 x 12 in)
chicken wire
Mossing wire
1.5 kg (3 lb) mistletoe
40 sprigs flowering ivy
18 wired tangerines
(SEE PAGE 61)
3 m (10 ft) star-printed
white ribbon

Gilt-edged
white ribbon
with gold stars

METHOD
Push the corners of the foam in, to make
a rough sphere. Wrap the chicken wire
around it and secure with mossing wire.
Attach several lengths of mossing wire to
the top of the sphere for extra strength
and hang, so you can work on it easily.
Stick sprigs of mistletoe and ivy into the
foam to completely cover. Wire in the
tangerines. Decorate with a bow at the
bottom (SEE PAGES 96–97), and twist
matching ribbon around the hanging wire.

Fir Lantern

To give your home a wonderfully old-fashioned feel, make an evergreen lantern lit with glowing candles. As with the traditional lanterns made in Victorian times, hang it in a window, to be enjoyed from both outside and inside the house. Alternatively, suspend it in a hallway or stairwell, where it can be viewed from all angles. As the candles burn down, their flames get closer to the foliage: to reduce the risk of fire, be present while the lantern is alight.

Sturdy chain •

• Miniature parcel

Small, pine cone •

Glowing Evergreens
A simple, green lantern constructed from rings of fir and four long-lasting candles. To make a larger lantern that can hold more candles, use bigger rings and add one more vertical ring for stability.

Metallic red
ribbon

Long-lasting candle

WHAT YOU NEED

*Two 152 x 15 cm (60 x 6 in)
chicken wire
160 x 15 cm (63 x 6 in)
chicken wire
30 handfuls damp moss
60 sprigs long-lasting conifer,
such as white fir, yew, or thuja
Mossing wire
3 m (10 ft) ribbon
Sturdy chain
4 pronged candle holders
4 candles
36 small, wired decorations,
eg. pine cones and miniature,
wrapped parcels*

METHOD

Make 3 moss frames,
one larger than the
others (SEE RIGHT).
Twine ribbon around
each. Holding the 2
small rings vertically,
push one through the other,
to form a sphere. Bind tightly with
mossing wire. Holding the larger ring
horizontally, slip it over the small rings
to complete your sphere. Bind firmly.
Wire a sturdy chain to the top of the
sphere for hanging. Stick the pronged
candle holders (with their candles) into the horizontal
ring, and secure. Finally, wire in the decorations.

CHICKEN-WIRE FRAME

CHICKEN-WIRE FRAMES filled with moss make strong,
adjustable bases for many of my wreaths. Larger
pieces of chicken wire can also be cut, filled with
moss, and stitched together for solid shapes
(SEE PAGES 26–27 AND 60–61).

1 Lay the chicken wire
flat. Arrange most of the moss
in a straight row down the length of
the chicken wire.

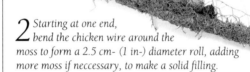

2 Starting at one end,
bend the chicken wire around the
moss to form a 2.5 cm- (1 in-) diameter roll, adding
more moss if neccessary, to make a solid filling.

3 Bend the roll into a circle and cover with foliage, either
securing overlapping sprays in place with mossing wire, or
inserting wired evergreens (sprigs of foliage each with stub wire
wound tightly around the
stem) into the frame.
Attach the ends
with wire.

Silk Flower Garland

GARLANDING LENDS A TRADITIONALLY festive air to the home, trailing around a doorway, window, or fireplace, or twisting up a banister. Preparing a garland can take a great deal of time, but because this one is made from dried material and silk flowers you can construct it well in advance. After Christmas, if you take the garland down carefully and store it in a box in a dark, dry place, it will last for several seasons. A threaded garland like this one looks equally good when viewed from all sides.

What You Need

25 silk, hydrangea
flower heads
Glue
Forty 2.5 cm (1 in)
cardboard circles
Large-eyed, darning needle
4 m (12 ft) green, garden
twine
1 matchstick
1.5 kg (3 lb) large, round,
dried leaves

Method

Cut the hydrangea florets so that there are just 2 or 3 on linked stems. Glue these to the outsides of cardboard circles to make a ruffle around the edges. Conceal the stalks with silk leaves. Make a hole in the centre of each piece of cardboard.

Thread the darning needle with twine and tie a matchstick on the end. Push the needle through 10 dried leaves at a time, pulling them down to the end of the twine, and threading on a hydrangea circle intermittently. Repeat until the garland is complete.

EXOTIC RUFFLES

The soft, muted colours of
the hydrangea flowers and the ruffled
edges of the dried leaves complement
each other well, making an unusual
but sophisticated, festive decoration.
You could use other silk flowers
in different colours for the
garland, but the size and
shape of the hydrangeas is
particularly suitable.

Round, dried leaf •

Silk, hydrangea flower •

Fruit & Nut Tree

TRADITIONAL SWAGS OR FESTOONS are essentially thick ropes of plant material and decorations that you can hang on a wall, drape around the mantelpiece, or use to adorn windows, doorways, and arches. Hanging panels are similar, but more fun, because you can make them into any shape: a column, a basket, an oversized bow, a cornucopia (SEE PAGES 26–27), or a hanging tree. This tree panel hangs fairly flat against the wall, yet it is a good size, making it ideal for a room with no space for a traditional tree. Composed of silver fir, rich red apples, limes, and gilded walnuts, it will last for several weeks without flagging.

Other Colours
For a different colour scheme, use tangerines or small oranges, gilded pomegranates (SEE PAGE 26), pinky red lychees, and gilded Brazil or pecan nuts, all of which stay fresh throughout the festive season.

What You Need
Two 7 x 2 x 112 cm (1½ x ¾ x 45 in) wood slats
7 x 2 x 90 cm (1½ x ¾ x 36 in) wood slat
4 m x 30 cm (12 ft x 12 in)
chicken wire
Mossing wire
Large sack damp moss
100 sprigs wired, silver fir
1 strand white lights
20 wired, red apples
15 wired limes
60 wired and gilded walnuts
Piece of bark
Strong hook

Method
Nail the wood slats together to form a triangle. Tightly stretch chicken wire over one side of the frame. Secure with mossing wire. Place a thick layer of moss on the frame side of the chicken wire. Stretch and secure the remaining chicken wire over the moss, to sandwich it. Sew loops of mossing wire through the frame to hold the moss firm. Push the fir into one side of the frame to cover. Attach the lights across the back, poking the bulbs through to the front. Decorate with the wired fruit and nuts. Attach the bark to the base with mossing wire. Secure a hanging loop of mossing wire to the top and suspend from a strong hook.

WIRING TECHNIQUES

WIRE NUTS AND FRUIT so that you can fasten them easily in place on your arrangement.

⚜ WIRING & GILDING NUTS ⚜

*B*end one end of a stub wire into a zig zag. Attach the bent end to a nut, using fast-drying glue. When the glue is dry, spray the nut with gold paint. For a "distressed" effect, lightly spray a rich red over the gold, making sure some of the gold still shows through.

⚜ WIRING FRUIT ⚜

*B*end a hook in one end of a thick stub wire. Poke the straight end through the base of the fruit and pull it through until the hook pierces the fruit and holds it firm. The wire is not strong enough to hold the fruit unsupported, but when it is pulled and looped back through an arrangement, it should easily hold.

Woodland Swag

FOR CENTURIES, THE PEOPLE in northern climes have brought branches of evergreen foliage into the home for the Christmas season. To me, simple garlands and swags made with a variety of evergreens are as beautiful as any Christmas decoration. Garlands lend your rooms their delicious fragrance: sharp, tangy, and sometimes citrus-like. Furthermore, they do not need glitter, baubles, or bows to add to their intrinsic, but subtle, beauty.

Blue fir

Glycerined and dyed copper beech

Dried mushroom

Bottlebrush

SHADES OF GREEN

*Long-lasting blue fir and golden cypress form the
predominant foliage, adding blue and gold tints to the green.
The glycerined and dyed copper beech introduces a glimmer
of deep red. Bottlebrush leaves form delicate spikes
among the conifer foliage, and large, dried, flat
mushrooms and pine cones, which both have
wonderful shapes, give varying textures.*

Golden cypress •

Pine cone •

Fruiting ivy •

WHAT YOU NEED

*2.4 m x 15 cm (8 ft x 6 in)
chicken wire
15 handfuls damp or
dry moss
30 sprigs wired, glycerined
and dyed copper beech,
blue fir, bottlebrush,
fruiting ivy, and
golden cypress
20 pine cones
15 dried mushrooms
Stub wires*

METHOD

Make a moss-filled chicken-wire
roll (SEE PAGE 57, STEPS 1 AND 2).
Ideally, you should use damp
moss, unless you intend to hang
the swag against mat paint or
wallpaper. Bend the frame into a
swag shape. Stick overlapping
sprigs of wired foliage into the
swag. Do the 2 sides first, starting
at the bases. For the central part
of the swag, work from the middle
outwards. Wire the pine cones and
mushrooms with stub wire, and attach.

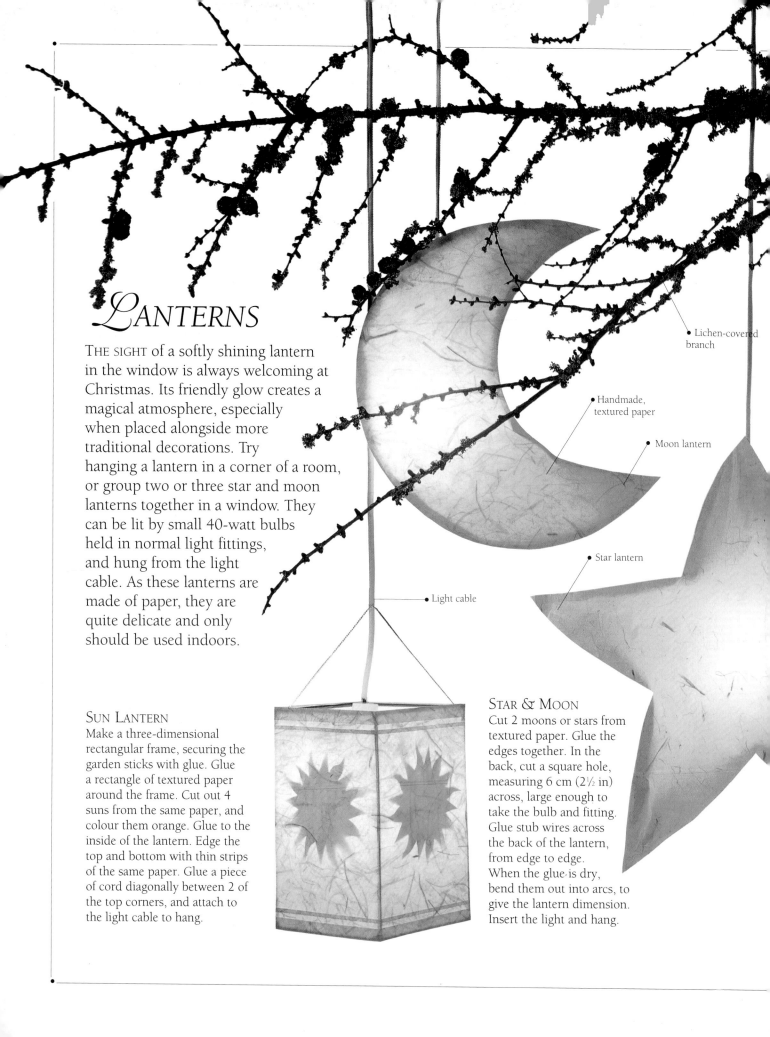

LANTERNS

THE SIGHT of a softly shining lantern in the window is always welcoming at Christmas. Its friendly glow creates a magical atmosphere, especially when placed alongside more traditional decorations. Try hanging a lantern in a corner of a room, or group two or three star and moon lanterns together in a window. They can be lit by small 40-watt bulbs held in normal light fittings, and hung from the light cable. As these lanterns are made of paper, they are quite delicate and only should be used indoors.

Lichen-covered branch

Handmade, textured paper

Moon lantern

Star lantern

Light cable

SUN LANTERN
Make a three-dimensional rectangular frame, securing the garden sticks with glue. Glue a rectangle of textured paper around the frame. Cut out 4 suns from the same paper, and colour them orange. Glue to the inside of the lantern. Edge the top and bottom with thin strips of the same paper. Glue a piece of cord diagonally between 2 of the top corners, and attach to the light cable to hang.

STAR & MOON
Cut 2 moons or stars from textured paper. Glue the edges together. In the back, cut a square hole, measuring 6 cm (2½ in) across, large enough to take the bulb and fitting. Glue stub wires across the back of the lantern, from edge to edge. When the glue·is dry, bend them out into arcs, to give the lantern dimension. Insert the light and hang.

JAPANESE LANTERN

Make 2 squares, one from short and one from long garden sticks. Glue the smaller frame into the larger frame, to form a diamond inside a square when viewed from above. Glue long sheets of papers to the smaller frame, and shorter ones to the larger frame. Tie cord diagonally between 2 corners. Attach to the light.

● Hanging cord

PYRAMIDAL LANTERN

Glue the sticks together to form a pyramidal frame. Glue a triangle of paper around the frame, leaving the top open. Insert the light. Tie cord at the top to secure.

● Wooden, lantern frame

WHAT YOU NEED
Glue
Handmade, textured paper
40-watt light fitting
Cord
Sun Lantern
Eight 13 cm (5 in) garden sticks
Four 23 cm (9 in) garden sticks
Orange ink
Star & Moon Lantern
Stout stub wires
Pyramidal Lantern
Six 23 cm (9 in) garden sticks
Japanese Lantern
Four 18 cm (7 in) garden sticks
Four 28 cm (11 in) garden sticks

TRADITIONAL TREE

RED AND GREEN ARE the traditional colours of Christmas. Wonderfully vibrant when combined, they each seem to make the other richer, deeper, and more lustrous. Several weeks before the festive season begins, the shops are piled high with decorations in red and green. You can make your own Christmas stars, painted baubles, cranberry decorations, and fabric eggs, or have a mixture of home-made and "shop-bought", to deck the tree for a special, traditional Christmas.

CHRISTMAS STARS
Cut out stars from thick card or balsa wood. Paint red and green designs on both sides, and attach a loop for hanging.

PAINTED BAUBLES
Make your own hand-painted baubles. Attach thread loops to table tennis balls, before you paint them.

CRANBERRY SWAGS
Thread firm cranberries on to long lengths of cotton, knotted at the end.

WHAT YOU NEED
For a 1.8 m (6 ft) tree:
41 cm- (16 in-) diameter terracotta pot
2 strands red, candle, clip-on lights
40 swathed Christmas eggs
20 cranberry spheres
20 Christmas stars
18 m (20 yd) cranberry swags
18 dried rose posies
15 painted baubles

FABRIC EGGS
Cover blown eggs with rich fabrics.

RUBY-RED SPHERES
A richly coloured sphere of cranberries adds its distinctive colour to the tree.

RICH, RED DECORATIONS

TIME IS INVARIABLY SHORT around Christmas, so make the swathed Christmas eggs well ahead, and store until needed. The cranberry spheres, however, need to be made about one week before Christmas.

SWATHED CHRISTMAS EGGS

1 Cut out a square of raw silk, large enough to draw around a blown egg. Gather one side of the square and tie with red thread, leaving ends to make a hanging loop.

2 Place the egg on the silk, with the narrow part at the gathered end. Stitch up the open side of the material bag.

3 Gather the material at the top of the egg, and finish by tying a bow with gold cord.

CRANBERRY SPHERES

1 Insert the straight end of a bent stub wire into a 1.5 cm- (¾in-) diameter foam ball. Pull through, threading a loop under the hook before pulling tight. Cut off the protruding wire, leaving 2 cm (¾ in) to bend back into the foam.

2 Glue cranberries on to the ball, positioning them as closely together as possible to leave no gaps. These cranberry spheres last about 2 weeks.

DRIED ROSE POSIES
Small bunches of dried roses and preserved ivy leaves secured with bows make unusual tree decorations (SEE PAGE 71).

What You Need

For a 1.8 m (6 ft) tree:
51 cm- (20 in-) square tub
2 strands white lights
45 iridescent icicles
20 miniature presents
20 silver stars
20 red berries
15 glittering glass balls
12 silvered pine cones
12 silver, glass cones
12 silver bows
9 m (10 yd) paper chains
10 white spheres

Painted Cones
Pine cones are a beautiful shape and a natural choice for decorating fir trees.

White Spheres
Spheres come in all colours. These snowballs are decorated with sprigs of holly.

Iridescent Icicles
The long, pointed shapes of these realistic, glass icicles give the tree strong definition.

Stars
Paint egg white on to glass stars, and sprinkle with glitter to create a frosted effect.

Tiny Gifts
Cover little boxes with silver paper, and add trimmings.

Silver Tree

CHOOSE A DESIGN THEME for your Christmas tree, using just one or two colours. Silver, reminiscent of frost, ice, and snow, makes the tree shimmer with cold. Tiny points of red accentuate the chill.

Silver Bows
Tie wire-edged silver ribbon into extravagant, eye-catching bows (SEE PAGES 96–97).

Glittering Glass Balls
Clear glass balls, patterned with a tracery of shimmering silver, glisten with reflections from the tree lights.

Glass Cones
The early Victorians decorated their trees with beautiful glass baubles. These cones are based on a traditional design.

TWISTED CHAINS
Metallic paper chains, twirled around the tree, catch the light on their many facets.

RED BERRIES
Twist artificial, wired berries to the tree to add drops of fiery red.

—✂— SILVERED PINE CONES ✂—

1 Bend a length of stub wire around the pine cone, near its base, leaving one end long enough for securing the cone to the

2 Twist the wire tightly around the cone to secure. Spray the cone with silver paint. While the paint is still wet, sprinkle with silver glitter. Do this job outdoors, preferably spraying into an old box.

SILVER DECORATIONS

WHILE YOU CAN BUY a host of silver decorations from the shops, it is fun to make some of the easier ones, such as the paper chains and silvered pine cones, yourself.

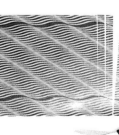

—✂— PAPER CHAINS ✂—

1 Choose 2 different sheets of silver wrapping paper and glue them back to back, so that the attractive sides show. Cut the paper into 2 cm (¾ in) strips.

2 Attach a piece of double-sided sticky tape to one end of each paper strip. Make a loop with a single twist in it. Thread each through the previous loop to make a chain.

DRIED FLOWER TREE

DRIED FLOWERS COMBINE TO make a surprisingly colourful tree. The paper bows enhance and strengthen the shades of the flowers while strands of matching raffia drift in a spiral up the tree, creating a swirl of movement.

SPRAY OF SCARLET ROSES
Red and green are opposing colours, so you will find that the impact of the little scarlet roses is strengthened by the backdrop of rich, dark green leaves. Pink heightens the drama.

COLOURED RAFFIA
Colour raffia with spray paints. Do this outside on a still day. Place 30–40 strands of raffia in a large, old box. Spray into the box, turning the strands so that they are coloured all over. Pull the raffia through the tree, allowing strands to catch on the branches.

OPULENT PEONY
A single, large, pink peony nestling among its own leaves makes a striking decoration. If the peony looks a little jaded, revive it with a burst of steam from a kettle, and blow it back into shape.

MOODY LARKSPURS
Deep mauve-blue larkspurs tied with a lilac ribbon strongly contrast with the other dried flowers on the tree.

HEADY HYDRANGEAS
Deep, plummy red hydrangeas, preserved in glycerine to which dye has been added, are tied together with glycerined ivy leaves and a lilac bow.

SUMMER ROSES
I have combined these yellow roses (still vibrant with summer colour) with ivy leaves, and introduced contrast with a blue-pink paper bow.

DRIED ROSES
Pink roses and a red bow work together wonderfully, each making the other more intense.

CAMPION
Dried pink campion retains a fresh look. An aquamarine bow accents its colour.

WHAT YOU NEED
For a 1.8 m (6 ft) tree:
46 cm- (18 in-) square fibreglass container
2 strands coloured lights
60 dried posy decorations
Five 1.2 m (4 ft) bundles coloured raffia

AIR-DRIED FLOWERS

1 Choose flowers with firm, well-shaped flowerheads for air-drying. Remove any leaves and flowers from the ends of the stems.

2 Tie 5 or 6 of the flowers together and hang in a cool, dark place until dry.

DRIED FLOWER DECORATIONS

BUNDLES OF DRIED FLOWERS and ivy leaves are simple to arrange. Make the bows in several colours of paper ribbon and tie them to the flower bunches. Use their binding wire to hang them from the Christmas tree.

DRIED POSY DECORATIONS

1 Gather a few dried flowers of your choice. Here I have used helichrysum. Add a few glycerined ivy leaves and arrange in a small posy.

2 Place a stub wire under the posy. Bend down a short end of wire to run parallel with the stems. Tightly twist the rest of the wire around the stems, just below the leaves. This makes the binding extra secure.

3 Make a single bow out of paper ribbon (SEE PAGES 96–97). Tie the bow on to the posy with a thin piece of the same ribbon.

MEXICAN TREE

MEXICO IS A COUNTRY of vibrant, shocking colours – the hottest reds, the most vicious pinks, vivid yellows and golds, and jewel-like greens and blues. Cover your tree with these clashing colours to add Latin heat to the home at Christmas.

DAZZLING HEARTS
Choose the brightest, metallic, wrapping papers you can find for making paper hearts. Combine reds and pinks, violets and oranges, and greens and blues to achieve a riotous colour scheme.

FLASHY SPHERES
Lightweight and inexpensive, tissue balls are simple to make. They are also showy with their mixed frills of the brightest colours.

RED-HOT CHAINS
Wear rubber gloves to string chillies as the juice can sting. The effort is well worth it, for they look enchanting among the branches.

TIN DECORATIONS
Search the shops for shiny, Mexican decorations made of painted tin cut into shapes of butterflies, birds, cockerels and chickens, fish, fruit, moons, stars, and suns. They are surprisingly inexpensive.

TINSEL TUFTS
Cut 1 cm (½ in) tufts off lengths of bright tinsel. Perch on the ends of branches to glitter like little mirrors as they reflect the Christmas tree lights.

WHAT YOU NEED

For a 1.8 m (6 ft) tree:
38 cm- (15 in-) diameter terracotta pot
2 strands white lights
7 m (8 yd) chilli chains
35 tin decorations
25 tissue balls
15 paper hearts
1 m (3 ft) star tinsel

MEXICAN PAPER DECORATIONS

TISSUE PAPERS AND SHINY, metallic, wrapping papers are available in a great range of designs. Make decorations in the brightest colours to convey a Mexican theme.

✂ TISSUE BALLS ✂

1 Place three 51 x 38 cm (20 x 15 in) rectangles of tissue paper on top of each other. Roughly pleat them, gathering the paper with the thumb and 2 fingers of each hand. Repeat with 3 more pieces of tissue paper.

2 Twist and scrunch the pleated papers. Pull them straight, and cut each into 13 cm (5 in) lengths with scissors or pinking shears.

3 Take 5 lengths, and tie them around the middle with wire or thread. Make a loop for hanging. Separate and tease the layers of tissue paper apart to form a ball.

✂ PAPER HEARTS ✂

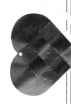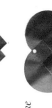

1 Use the template on page 116 to cut out 2 shapes from metallic paper. Fold each in half. Make 2 or more cuts, from the folded edge to the start of the curved section.

2 Weave the strips of the 2 shapes together, to

3 Use a hole puncher to make a hole just below the "V" of the heart, and attach a loop of cord or ribbon for hanging.

Japanese Tree

Japanese design and packaging are arguably the best in the world, and their use of paper is innovative. At first, origami is a challenge but, with practice, it becomes easier. Children learn quickly, and soon rattle off these kimonos.

What You Need
For a 1.8 m (6 ft) tree:
51 cm- (20 in-) square tub
2 strands coloured lights
30 paper fans
30 origami kimonos
30 paper lanterns on sticks
30 papered boxes
20 paper lanterns
20 papier mâché masks
15 bird ornaments

Face Masks
Warriors' faces are painted in brilliant colours on papier mâché masks.

Paper Fans
Pleated fans are made from origami paper.

Lanterns
These lanterns help to break the tree's outline.

Improvise!
Use colourful parasols sold for cocktail decorations to adorn this tree.

Oriental Light
Paper lanterns are sold packed flat, but pull out like a concertina.

Birds
Coloured birds sit among the branches or swing on perches.

Paper Kimonos
Use decorative papers for handmade kimonos.

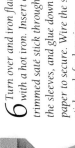

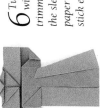

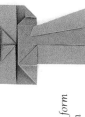

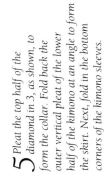

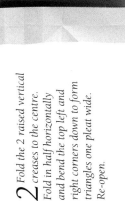

TAPERED BOXES
Cover matchboxes with Japanese paper to emphasize the Japanese theme.

ORIGAMI KIMONOS

1 Fold a 23 cm (9 in) square of origami paper in half vertically. Unfold. Pleat vertically into 8 as shown. Unfold. Pleat the top half horizontally into 4, as shown. Unfold.

2 Fold the 2 raised vertical creases to the centre. Fold in half horizontally and bend the top left and right corners down to form triangles one pleat wide. Re-open.

3 Turn the sheet over and form a small diamond by pushing in the top 2 corners of the raised section, and fold down as shown.

4 Turn the paper over and bend the top pleat down. Lift the top of the diamond up from the back, and pleat the central horizontal fold up. Fold the outer vertical edges into the centre; the triangles from step 2 will bend into place.

5 Pleat the top half of the diamond in 3, as shown, to form the collar. Fold back the outer vertical pleat of the lower half of the kimono at an angle to form the skirt. Next, fold in the bottom corners of the kimono sleeves.

6 Turn over and iron flat with a hot iron. Insert a trimmed saté stick through the sleeves, and glue down the paper to secure. Wire the saté stick ends for hanging.

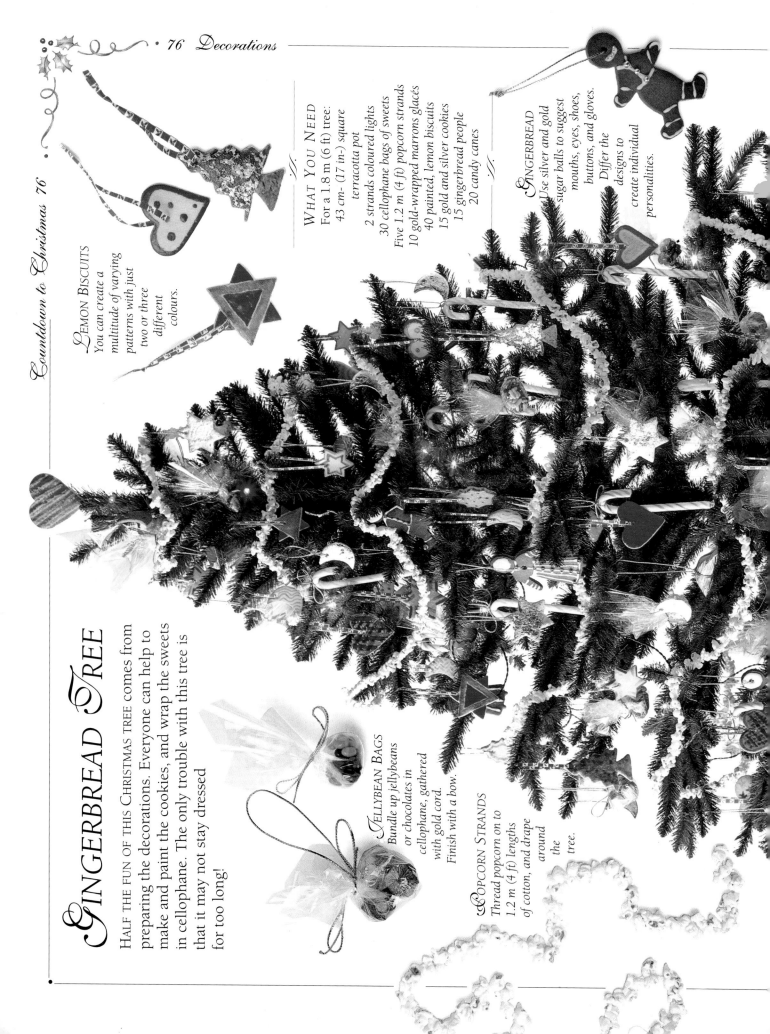

GINGERBREAD TREE

HALF THE FUN OF THIS CHRISTMAS TREE comes from preparing the decorations. Everyone can help to make and paint the cookies, and wrap the sweets in cellophane. The only trouble with this tree is that it may not stay dressed for too long!

WHAT YOU NEED
For a 1.8 m (6 ft) tree:
43 cm- (17 in-) square terracotta pot
2 strands coloured lights
30 cellophane bags of sweets
Five 1.2 m (4 ft) popcorn strands
10 gold-wrapped marrons glacés
40 painted, lemon biscuits
15 gold and silver cookies
15 gingerbread people
20 candy canes

LEMON BISCUITS
You can create a multitude of varying patterns with just two or three different colours.

GINGERBREAD
Use silver and gold sugar balls to suggest mouths, eyes, shoes, buttons, and gloves. Differ the designs to create individual personalities.

JELLYBEAN BAGS
Bundle up jellybeans or chocolates in cellophane, gathered with gold cord. Finish with a bow.

POPCORN STRANDS
Thread popcorn on to 1.2 m (4 ft) lengths of cotton, and drape around the tree.

CANDY CANES
You can either hook these colourfully twirled candy canes over the branches, or hang them from gold cord.

PAINTED BISCUITS

1 Paint the unbaked, lemon biscuit with egg-yolk glazes in your choice of colours (SEE PAGE 80).

2 After the biscuit is baked, it will have a shiny, translucent glaze. When cool and hard, thread a loop of ribbon or cord through the hole.

EDIBLE ADORNMENTS

BAKE THE BISCUITS reasonably hard to prevent them from crumbling. Make holes for hanging before baking, large enough for you to thread through a piece of ribbon.

GINGERBREAD PEOPLE

1 Make a cone with a very pointed end from a rectangular piece of greaseproof paper. Tape to secure. Fill with stiff icing made from icing sugar and water, and tear or cut a tiny hole across the tip, for drawing.

2 Squeeze the piping cone to force out the icing. Draw lines and blobs to suggest clothes and facial features.

3 While the icing is still soft, position sugar balls to form eyes, mouths, buttons, and decorative edgings. Allow the icing to set before threading cord through the hole.

GOLD & SILVER COOKIES
Paint a baked cookie with egg white, then gently float a sheet of gold or silver on to it.

CHRISTMAS TREE QUARTET

IF YOU HAVE A CLIPPED TREE growing in a pot out in your garden, bring it inside for Christmas. Box, bay, yew, hemlock, privet, and holly all can be grown in containers and adapted as Christmas trees for the holiday season. Alternatively, make a mock mop-head (SEE BELOW) from sprigs of holly and a chicken-wire frame.

Top-knot Tree
WHAT YOU NEED
Clipped box tree
*30 cm- (12 in-) diameter
terracotta pot*
6 handfuls silver lichen
30 red, fabric roses, in 3 sizes
3 m (10 ft) gathered, red ribbon
1 strand white lights

TOP-KNOT TREE
A box tree trained into two top-knots makes an extraordinary Christmas tree. Set off the rich, dark green, tiny leaves with red roses and twirls of ribbon, and use white lights to add pinpoints of brightness.

Variagated holly

White light

Mop-headed Holly
WHAT YOU NEED
*51 x 30 cm (20 x 12 in)
chicken wire*
*20 cm- (8 in-) diameter foam
ball, soaked*
Mossing wire
41 cm- (16 in-) diameter plastic pot
Plaster of Paris mix
1.2 m (4 ft) branch
46 cm- (18 in-) diameter decorative pot
3 handfuls carpet moss
120 sprigs holly
1 strand white lights

Clipped
box tree

Gathered, red ribbon

Carpet moss

Silver lichen

MOP-HEADED HOLLY
Wrap chicken wire around the foam. Secure with mossing wire. Fill the plastic pot with wet plaster of Paris, and set the branch into it. When the plaster is dry, put the pot in the decorative pot. Cover the plaster with moss. Spike the sphere on to the branch and cover with holly. Decorate with lights.

Perfect Pyramid
WHAT YOU NEED
Neat, pyramidal conifer
61 cm- (24 in-) square
lead container
40 baubles
15 tissue-paper flowers
(SEE PAGES 22–23)
1 strand coloured lights

Owl decoration

Bay tree

Robin decoration

Tissue-paper flower

Neat, pyramidal conifer

Silver bauble

Gold bauble

Multi-coloured bauble

PERFECT PYRAMID
The dense foliage of this conifer pyramid is adorned with hot-pink, tissue-paper flowers, harlequin and silver baubles, and a strand of coloured lights to make a sophisticated Christmas tree.

Bay Tree of Birds
WHAT YOU NEED
Bay tree
51 cm- (20 in-) square terracotta pot
15 handfuls bun moss
10 multi-coloured baubles
10 gold baubles
1 strand white lights
7 robin decorations
3 owl decorations

BAY TREE OF BIRDS
The simple beauty of this delicate bay tree is enhanced by its plaited stem. I chose glittering, textured sequins and shiny baubles to complement the almost mat-like surface of the leaves, while robins and owls add a whimsical touch.

Harlequin bauble

Bun moss

Lead container

Square terracotta pot

COOKIE SELECTION

TEA TIME HAS ALWAYS been a great family occasion although, over the festive season, food is usually so plentiful that only cups of tea and biscuits are welcome. Simple lemon and ginger biscuits are perfect, decorated with either icing and sugar balls or bright colour glazes, a job that children love. Tempting, bite-size wreaths, topped with cherries and gold and silver sugar balls, are show stoppers, so is the sticky nut brittle. More elegant delicacies include brandy snaps tipped with bitter chocolate and filled with whipped cream; rich, chocolate Florentines; and tiny tartlets piled with glazed fruits.

NUT BRITTLE

455 g (1 lb) mixed pistachios, cashews,
*   almonds, and hazelnuts*
455 g (1 lb) caster sugar

Toast the nuts and arrange them in a 33 x 23 cm (13 x 9 in) greased baking tin. Slowly melt the sugar in a heavy saucepan over a low heat, stirring all the time until it is liquid but not caramelized. Pour the syrup over the nuts; do not stir. When the brittle is cold, unmould it, and cut or break into pieces. Makes 18.

LEMON BISCUITS

115 g (4 oz) butter
85 g (3 oz) caster sugar
Grated rind of 1 lemon
170 g (6 oz) plain flour
1 egg yolk (size 2) and food colouring
*   to glaze*

Cream the butter and sugar until fluffy. Stir in the lemon rind and flour. Roll the dough to 3 mm (⅛ in) thickness and cut with biscuit cutters. Make holes for hanging the biscuits, if you like. Place on a greased baking tray. Divide the egg yolk between 3 small bowls, and add ½ tsp different food colouring to each. Paint the biscuits and bake at 175° C (350° F) for 12 minutes, until lightly browned. Makes 40.

Fruit Tartlet

Nut Brittle

Toasted nuts

Egg glaze

Lemon Biscuit

FRUIT TARTLETS

60 g (2 oz) caster sugar
1 egg and 1 egg yolk (size 3)
30 g (1 oz) cornflour
590 ml (1 pt) milk
½ tsp vanilla essence
340 g (¾ lb) shortcrust pastry
Lightly poached fruit and apricot jam

Make the custard. Whisk the sugar, egg, and egg yolk until light and fluffy. Whisk in the cornflour, and then the milk and vanilla essence. Bring the mixture just below boiling in a saucepan over a low heat. Stir constantly for 2 minutes, until the custard coats the back of a spoon. Cover with a piece of greaseproof paper and leave to cool.

Roll the pastry to 3 mm (⅛ in) thickness. Line small, greased tartlet tins with the pastry and bake blind at 200° C (400° F) for 15 minutes. When the pastry is cool, spoon custard into each tartlet. Arrange the lightly poached fruit on top of each tartlet, and glaze with warm apricot jam. Makes 30.

FLORENTINES

170 g (6 oz) baking chocolate
130 g (4½ oz) mixture of toasted
    almonds, hazelnuts, and pecans;
    glacé cherries; kumquats; orange
    and lemon peel; and crystallized
    violets

Melt the chocolate in a bowl
over a saucepan of simmering
water. Pour tablespoonfuls of
chocolate on to greaseproof
paper. Arrange nuts, fruit, peel,
and crystallized violets on the
chocolate before it sets. Peel off
the paper when the florentines
have set. Makes 15.

COOKIE WREATHS

85 g (3 oz) butter
170 g (6 oz) marshmallows
4 drops vanilla essence
1 tsp green food colouring
115 g (4 oz) cornflakes
Glacé cherries and silver and gold
    sugar balls to decorate

Melt the butter in a heavy saucepan
over a low heat. Add the marshmallows
and stir until melted. Stir in the vanilla
essence and food colouring, then mix
in the cornflakes. Drop tablespoonfuls of the mixture on to greaseproof paper and press a hole in
the middle of each. Decorate
while still soft. Makes 12.

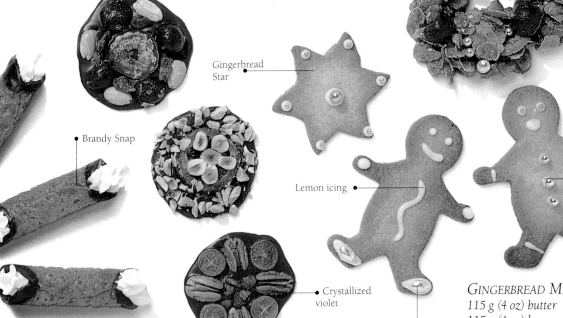

Cookie Wreath

Glacé cherry

Gingerbread
Star

Lemon icing

Crystallized
violet

Sugar ball

Florentine

Brandy Snap

Whipped
cream

Gingerbread
Man

BRANDY SNAPS

170 g (6 oz) unsalted butter
230 g (8 oz) golden syrup
60 g (2 oz) sugar
1 tsp ground ginger
170 g (6 oz) plain flour
1 tbs brandy
Melted chocolate and whipped
    cream to serve

Place the first 4 ingredients in a
saucepan and bring to the boil, stirring

constantly. Beat in the flour and
brandy. Drop tablespoonfuls on to a
greased baking tray, at 10 cm (4 in)
intervals. Bake at 175° C (350° F) for
8 minutes. Allow to cool for 1 minute,
then roll each biscuit around a greased
wooden-spoon handle. If the biscuits
harden while shaping, return them to
the oven. When cooled, dip the ends
in melted chocolate. Just before
serving, pipe whipped cream into
the centres. Makes 25.

GINGERBREAD MEN & STARS

115 g (4 oz) butter
115 g (4 oz) brown sugar
85 g (3 oz) treacle
1 egg (size 3)
285 g (10 oz) plain flour
1 tsp baking powder
2 tsp ground ginger
1 tsp ground cinnamon
Lemon icing and sugar balls to decorate

Cream the butter and sugar. Add the
treacle and egg, and mix until smooth.
Stir in the flour, baking powder, and
spices, and mix to form a stiff dough.
Chill for 1 hour. Roll out to 3 mm
(⅛ in) thickness and cut with biscuit
cutters. Place on a greased baking tray
and bake at 175° C (350° F) for 10
minutes. When cool, decorate with
lemon icing and sugar balls. Makes 35.

Sugared Flowers & Fruit

CHRISTMAS IS THE SEASON to indulge in exceedingly sweet treats. Sugared flowers and fruits sparkle under a crisp dusting of crystals that shimmer enticingly in the light and tingle on the tongue. A surprising number of flowers and leaves are delicious to eat: roses, primroses, pansies, fruit tree blossoms, mimosa flowers, not to mention the numerous varieties of mint, which are particularly good. Whole or sectioned fruit under a veil of sugar also make beautiful decorations, until you can resist them no longer.

WHAT YOU NEED
1 egg white
Small paintbrush
230 g (8 oz) edible flowers, leaves, and fruit
85 g (3 oz) granulated sugar

METHOD
Lightly beat the egg white. Using a paintbrush, cover the surfaces of each flower, leaf, or fruit with egg white, taking care not to saturate. Place on greaseproof paper and sieve sugar over to cover evenly. Let dry in a warm place for 2 to 3 hours. Sugared this way, flowers last in perfect condition for several days, and fruit keeps as long as when it is fresh.

Kumquat

Lime

Black fig

Red plum

Turkish delight

FLORAL SWEETS
Decorate bought or homemade fruit-and-nut nougat with delicately sugared rose petals and primrose flowers.

Nougat

PYRAMID OF FRUIT
Large red plums, luscious black figs, limes (to squeeze over the figs), and sharp, bite-sized kumquats make up the glistening pyramid of delicately sugared fruit. Choose only the most perfect-looking fruits for the arrangement.

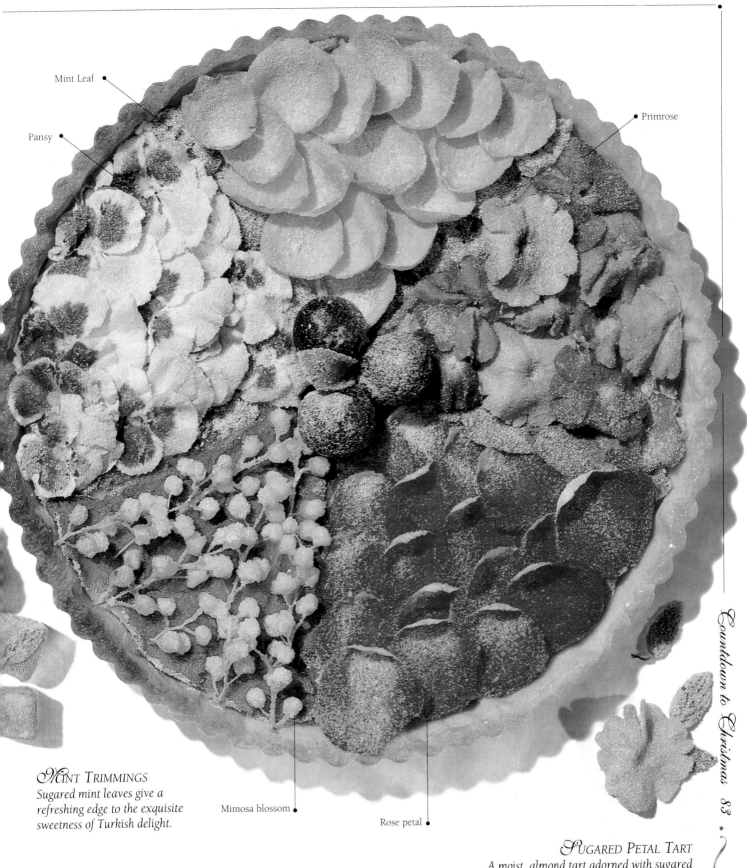

Mint Leaf

Pansy

Primrose

Mimosa blossom

Rose petal

MINT TRIMMINGS
*Sugared mint leaves give a
refreshing edge to the exquisite
sweetness of Turkish delight.*

SUGARED PETAL TART
*A moist, almond tart adorned with sugared
pansies, mimosa, primroses, and rose petals.
Arranged in the form of a flower, each of its
five "petals" is edged with sugared mint leaves.*

Swaying Jellies

JELLIES ARE A GREATLY underrated dessert. I'd like to elevate homemade jellies to a place near the top of the pudding hierarchy. They can be as refreshing and cool as a sorbet, or as rich and creamy as a mousse. Made in a decorative mould, they can also look astounding. A few little-known techniques are essential for a perfect result. Before making the jelly, oil the mould liberally and place it in the refrigerator for at least one hour. To prepare the gelatin, soften it in cold water, without stirring, for five minutes. When spongy, heat carefully until melted, shaking gently without stirring. For large or tall moulds, use a little more gelatin for extra stability, but not too much or the wobble will be spoilt.

Copper mould

Port Jelly

Wickedly Special
We were always treated to a port jelly at Christmas in my childhood. At the time, it seemed such a special treat – because it was alcoholic.

Fantasy Moulds
Many amazingly shaped, copper moulds were made for ice creams and jellies at the beginning of this century. If you cannot find any, choose from the immense range of ceramic moulds available.

Port Jelly
20 g (¾ oz) gelatin in 90 ml (3 fl oz) water
Grated rind and juice of 1 large lemon
355 ml (12 fl oz) water
½ cinnamon stick
4 cloves
170 g (6 oz) caster sugar
295 ml (10 fl oz) port
60 g (2 oz) fresh, or crystallized cranberries (SEE PAGES 38–39)

Prepare the gelatin (SEE ABOVE). Place the lemon rind and juice, water, cinnamon, cloves, and caster sugar in a saucepan and bring to the boil. Remove from the heat and add the melted gelatin. Let cool for 20 minutes, then stir in the port. Strain, and allow to almost set.

Pour half of the jelly into a prepared 890 ml (30 fl oz) mould and float the cranberries on the surface. Refrigerate until set. Pour the remaining jelly over the cranberry layer. Refrigerate overnight. Remove 2 hours before serving; unmould an hour before. Serves 6.

FLUMMERY

30 g (1 oz) gelatin in 120 ml
  (4 fl oz) water
Grated rind and juice of
  1 lemon
4 eggs (size 3)
60 g (2 oz) caster sugar
475 ml (16 fl oz) dry sherry
A pinch of nutmeg

Prepare the gelatin (SEE LEFT),
then add cold water to make
up to 475 ml (16 fl oz). Stir
in the lemon rind and juice.
Mix the eggs, sugar, sherry,
and nutmeg, and add to the
melted gelatin. Heat in a
double boiler, until it coats
the back of a spoon. Strain
into an 890 ml (30 fl oz)
mould and refrigerate overnight. Remove 2 hours
before serving; unmould
an hour before. Serves 8.

Flummery

ANCIENT TASTE
Flummery, a very old recipe made with
rich sherry custard flavoured with lemon,
has a traditional, Christmas flavour.

MOCHA JELLY
Chocolate Jelly:
4 egg yolks (size 3)
115 g (4 oz) caster sugar
4 tbs cocoa powder
445 ml (¾ pt) milk
2 tbs rum
15 g (½ oz) gelatin in 60 ml
  (2 fl oz) water
150 ml (5 fl oz) whipping
  cream, whipped
Coffee Jelly:
445 ml (¾ pt) coffee
115 g (4 oz) caster sugar
15 g (½ oz) gelatin in 60 ml
  (2 fl oz) water
2 tbs coffee liqueur
Rum-flavoured cream to serve

Make the chocolate jelly.
Beat the egg yolks, sugar,
and cocoa powder until
creamy. Heat the milk to
just below boiling, then
whisk into the egg-yolk
mixture. Heat in a double-
boiler until it coats the back
of a spoon. Remove from the
heat and stir in the rum.
When cool, stir in the
melted gelatin (SEE LEFT).
Allow to almost set, then
fold in the whipped cream.
  Make the coffee jelly. Heat
the coffee and sugar. Stir in
the melted gelatin and coffee
liqueur and leave until it
is almost set. Pour half of
the chocolate jelly into a
prepared 890 ml (30 fl oz)
mould. Let set, then pour in
half of the coffee jelly. When
set, repeat to make 2 more
layers. Refrigerate overnight.
Remove 2 hours before
serving; unmold an
hour before. Pass
rum-flavoured
cream separately.
Serves 6.

Mocha Jelly

MOCHA FLAVOUR
Dark chocolate and coffee
jellies combine in layers to form
a cool and creamy mocha jelly with
a simply delicious flavour.

CHOCOLATE TRUFFLES

TRUFFLES, OF THE CHOCOLATE KIND, have to be one of the most delicious and wicked treats of all time. They seem more "chocolatey" than chocolate and "creamier" than cream. With the added flavours of brandy, rum, or another favourite liqueur, they are an indulgence that is absolutely essential at Christmas time. Shop-bought truffles are good, but these homemade ones are unforgettable. They can all be made a month in advance and frozen.

• Pink Champagne Truffles

• Rum Truffles dusted with icing sugar

VANILLA TRUFFLES

To make these truffles, follow the recipe for Cream Truffles, but add ½ tsp of vanilla essence instead of liqueur. You can then coat the truffles with melted white chocolate.

BUTTERY TRUFFLES

285 g (10 oz) baking chocolate
115 g (4 oz) unsalted butter
60 ml (2 fl oz) water
1 egg yolk (size 3), lightly beaten
1 tbs flavouring (brandy, rum, other liqueurs, or espresso coffee)
Cocoa powder, icing sugar, or instant coffee powder and icing sugar, to decorate

Break the chocolate into small pieces and heat with the butter and water in a double boiler, stirring until smooth. Stir in the egg yolk and flavouring. Pour into a 15 cm- (6 in-) square tin, lined with greaseproof paper. Refrigerate until set. Remove from the tin by the paper. Cut into squares, or mould into balls. Roll or dust the truffles in cocoa powder, icing sugar, or instant coffee powder and icing sugar. Refrigerate for a week or freeze for up to a month. Makes 35.

DOUBLE-DIPPED TRUFFLES

Cream Truffles flavoured with Grand Marnier are double-dipped in dark and white chocolate. Prepare two bowls of melted chocolate, one dark and one white. Skewer each truffle. Dip half in the white chocolate, let set, and then dip the other half in dark chocolate.

CREAM TRUFFLES

285 g (10 oz) baking chocolate
115 g (4 oz) unsalted butter
295 ml (½ pt) double cream
2 tbs flavouring (brandy, rum, other liqueurs, or espresso coffee)

Break the chocolate into small pieces and melt with the butter in a double boiler, stirring until smooth. Warm the cream just below boiling, and stir into the chocolate mixture. Add the flavouring and allow to cool. Freeze until solid. Remove from the freezer and scoop into balls, about 2 cm (¾ in) in diameter. Coat the truffles in melted chocolate (SEE ABOVE RIGHT) and allow to cool. Truffles will keep for a week in the refrigerator, or up to a month in the freezer. Makes 20.

RUM TRUFFLES

Buttery Truffles can be flavoured with dark rum, and rolled in cocoa powder.

PINK CHAMPAGNE TRUFFLES

Champagne-liqueur-flavoured Cream Truffles are coated in melted white chocolate, lightly tinted with pink food colouring.

COATING CREAM TRUFFLES

Prepare a bowl of melted dark or white chocolate. Skewer a cream truffle and dip it in the chocolate to coat completely. Lift it out, twirling the tail of chocolate to the side of the truffle. Slip the skewer through the wires of a rack until the truffle rests on it, then pull to remove the skewer. Repeat for the rest of the truffles.

• Cream Truffles dipped in dark chocolate

TIA MARIA TRUFFLES

The delicious coffee flavour of Tia Maria in the Buttery Truffles is echoed by a dusting of instant coffee powder mixed with icing sugar.

NUTTY TRUFFLES

Dip amaretto-flavoured Cream Truffles in melted chocolate mixed with broken, toasted almonds.

CHOCOLATE LILY

Melt 340 g (12 oz) white or dark chocolate and 3 tbs maple syrup in a double boiler. When cool, press into petal shapes. Pour 1 tsp melted chocolate into a teacup lined with plastic wrap. Slightly furl each chocolate petal and arrange in the cup: layer the petals from the outside inwards. Finish with two twirled petals in the centre. Remove the completed chocolate lily when set.

PETITS FOURS

PETITS FOURS, LITTLE SWEETMEATS eaten with coffee at the end of a meal, are perilous delights that lie somewhere between cakes and confectionery. The French king, Louis XVI, who is known to have enjoyed them, gave them their name ("little oven" in English). His petits fours were probably small, sponge cakes, but now they give their name to any small, sweet delicacies.

I have always liked fruit-based petits fours, because they clear the palate after a rich meal. Little, fluted biscuits filled with raspberries, and various fruit dipped in fondants and dark and white chocolates, are a perfect finale to a special dinner.

STUFFED PRUNES
Stuff Armagnac- or brandy-soaked prunes with apricot purée (SEE PAGE 37), or marzipan – make roses from thin strips rolled into coils.

RASPBERRIES IN TULIPES
Whisk 3 egg whites until just mixed. Stir in 200 g (7 oz) plain flour and 115 g (4 oz) icing sugar, then 115 g (4 oz) cooled, melted butter. Place teaspoonfuls of the batter on to a greased baking tray, and spread it as thinly as possible with the back of the spoon, to form 7.5 cm (3 in) circles. Bake at 220° C (425° F) for 3 minutes, until golden. Mould each biscuit over an upturned egg cup to form a fluted biscuit. Before serving, fill with raspberries dusted with icing sugar. Makes 40.

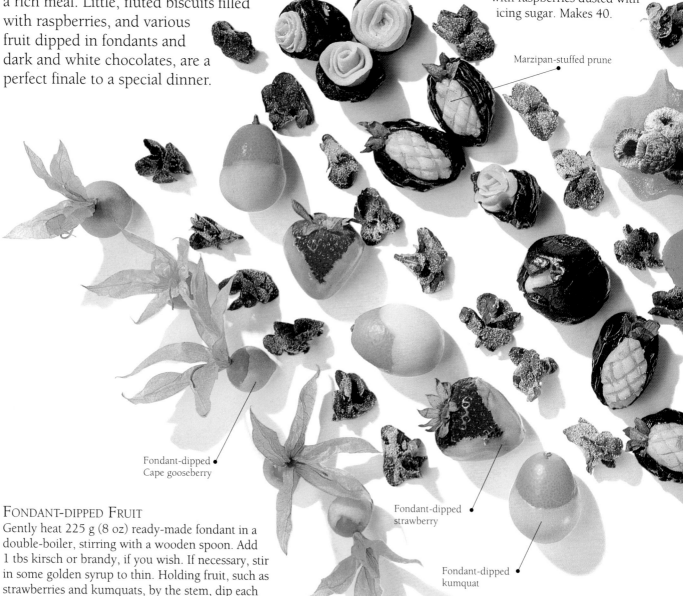

Marzipan-stuffed prune

Fondant-dipped
Cape gooseberry

Fondant-dipped
strawberry

Fondant-dipped
kumquat

FONDANT-DIPPED FRUIT
Gently heat 225 g (8 oz) ready-made fondant in a double-boiler, stirring with a wooden spoon. Add 1 tbs kirsch or brandy, if you wish. If necessary, stir in some golden syrup to thin. Holding fruit, such as strawberries and kumquats, by the stem, dip each piece into the fondant and place right side up on greaseproof paper, to set. Covers about 40.

CARAMEL PROFITEROLES & NUTS

Heat 115 g (4 oz) caster sugar and 4 tbs water in a saucepan, until golden. Place 12 profiteroles on a wire rack over greaseproof paper, and spoon the caramel over them. Place mounds of nuts on a marble slab and pour remaining syrup over them. Remove with a spatula when cool. Caramel petits fours are best eaten the day that they are made. Covers 12 profiteroles and 10 nut mounds.

DOUBLE-DIPPED FRUIT

Melt white chocolate in a double-boiler. Dip one side of fresh or crystallized fruit into it. Leave on greaseproof paper to set. Meanwhile, melt dark chocolate. Dip the other side of the fruit in the dark chocolate. Leave to set.

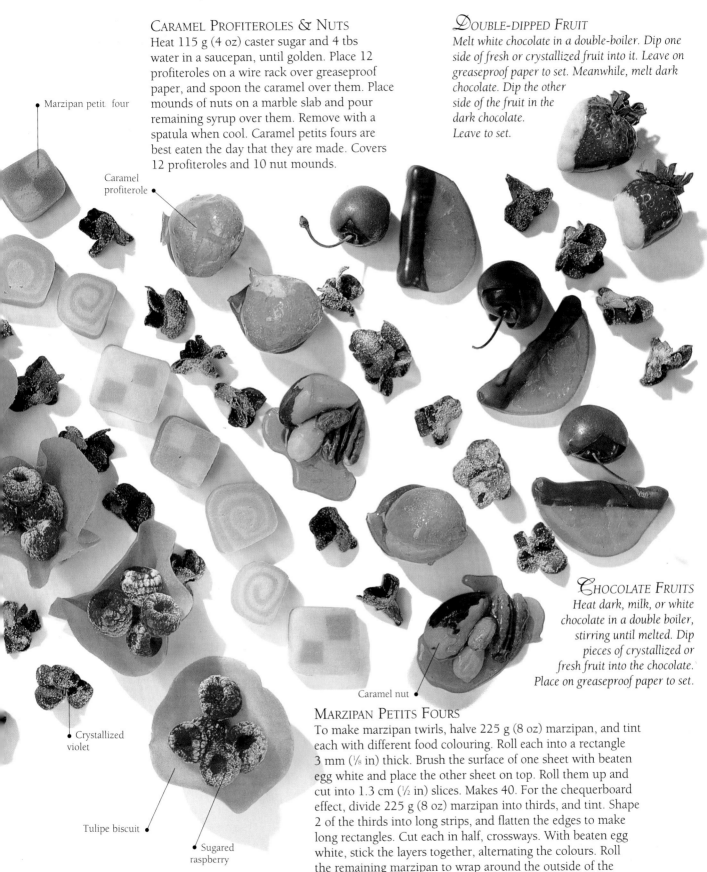

- Marzipan petit four
- Caramel profiterole
- Crystallized violet
- Tulipe biscuit
- Sugared raspberry
- Caramel nut

CHOCOLATE FRUITS

Heat dark, milk, or white chocolate in a double boiler, stirring until melted. Dip pieces of crystallized or fresh fruit into the chocolate. Place on greaseproof paper to set.

MARZIPAN PETITS FOURS

To make marzipan twirls, halve 225 g (8 oz) marzipan, and tint each with different food colouring. Roll each into a rectangle 3 mm (⅛ in) thick. Brush the surface of one sheet with beaten egg white and place the other sheet on top. Roll them up and cut into 1.3 cm (½ in) slices. Makes 40. For the chequerboard effect, divide 225 g (8 oz) marzipan into thirds, and tint. Shape 2 of the thirds into long strips, and flatten the edges to make long rectangles. Cut each in half, crossways. With beaten egg white, stick the layers together, alternating the colours. Roll the remaining marzipan to wrap around the outside of the chequered marzipan. Cut into 1.3 cm (½ in) slices. Makes 40.

Chapter Three

LAST-MINUTE CREATIONS

THE GREAT DAY has arrived. I find that it helps
to make a list of everything that needs to be
done – it is the only way that I remember to
arrange flowers waiting in a bucket, chill the
white wine, and serve the cheese or a salad I
have already made. It is certainly easier to
have the feast in the evening, so that there
is ample time for preparation. Remember,
the main aim is to enjoy the day, so have
plenty of happy helpers at hand.

FRESH AND FRAGRANT
Perfumed deep red and white roses, white tulips,
spicy-scented lilies, sprays of pale pink and gold
orchids, fatsia leaves, and the intriguing kangaroo
paw flowers spill out of a flared and fluted vase in
festive disarray. A starry background
dramatically offsets the arrangement.

Tartan Stockings

WHEN I WAS A CHILD, waiting for my stocking on Christmas Eve was almost unbearable. I slept fitfully and, consequently, was tired and rather bad-tempered on Christmas Day. My favourite stocking, the largest, was big enough to take a hefty present, as well as plenty of stocking fillers. At least one unwrapped present was always at the top, giving an exciting taster of what was to come!

Corals and Blue

A stocking in shades of coral pink and cornflower blue, with matching trim, bulges with hidden "goodies". A knitted Piglet, ears flying, waits anxiously to be picked up, while the ubiquitous tangerine will keep you going as you explore the stocking's contents.

Candy cane•

Seasonal Stripes

A teddy bear and tiny present peep from the top of this red and green striped stocking, tempting the recipient to look further. The stocking's stripes are quilted, with a cuff of horizontal stripes. A jolly, red and green bow and cord piping add a final flourish.

Rich Reds & Golds

This red and gold tartan stocking, quilted diagonally, has a cuff of bright red satin edged with satin cord. Inside, a toy soldier and twirled candy canes wait for some lucky child.

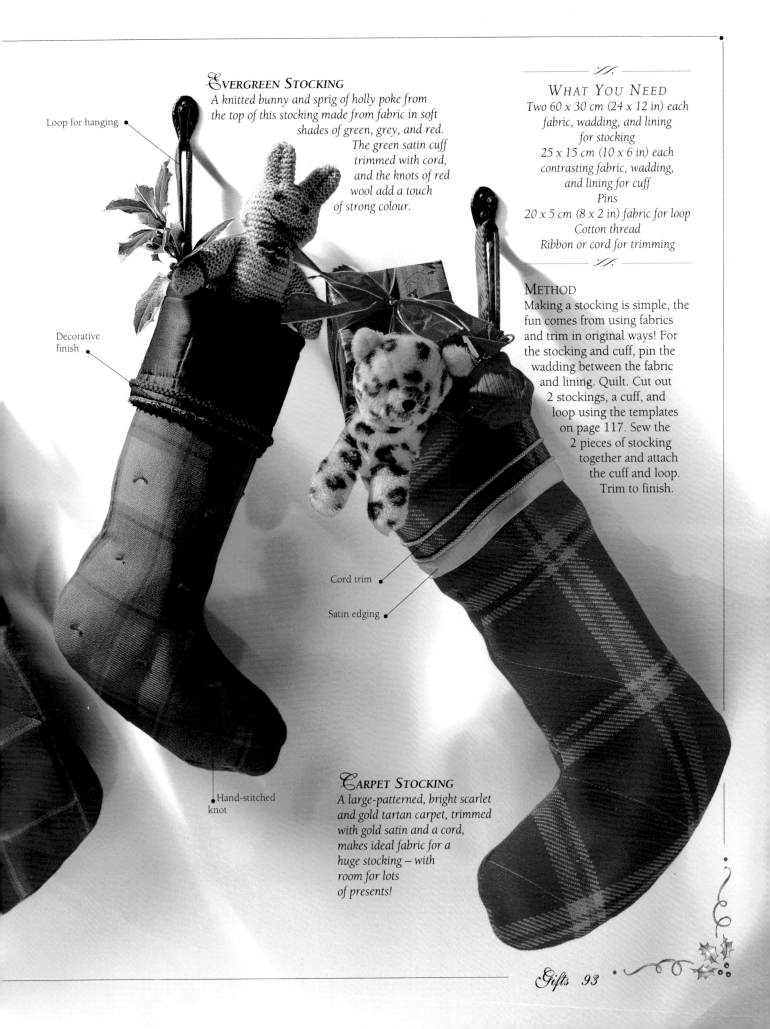

Evergreen Stocking

A knitted bunny and sprig of holly poke from the top of this stocking made from fabric in soft shades of green, grey, and red. The green satin cuff trimmed with cord, and the knots of red wool add a touch of strong colour.

Loop for hanging

Decorative finish

Hand-stitched knot

Cord trim

Satin edging

— ✄ —

WHAT YOU NEED

Two 60 x 30 cm (24 x 12 in) each fabric, wadding, and lining for stocking
25 x 15 cm (10 x 6 in) each contrasting fabric, wadding, and lining for cuff
Pins
20 x 5 cm (8 x 2 in) fabric for loop
Cotton thread
Ribbon or cord for trimming

— ✄ —

METHOD
Making a stocking is simple, the fun comes from using fabrics and trim in original ways! For the stocking and cuff, pin the wadding between the fabric and lining. Quilt. Cut out 2 stockings, a cuff, and loop using the templates on page 117. Sew the 2 pieces of stocking together and attach the cuff and loop. Trim to finish.

Carpet Stocking

A large-patterned, bright scarlet and gold tartan carpet, trimmed with gold satin and a cord, makes ideal fabric for a huge stocking – with room for lots of presents!

DECORATIVE GIFT BOXES

AMONG THE MULTITUDES OF GIFT BOXES in the shops, I recommend that you buy the more complicated ones, adding decorations of your own. Simpler boxes, however, are easy to prepare if you use the templates given (SEE PAGE 117). Paste your own choice of wrapping paper, or even decorative pages from a magazine, to the card used to make the boxes. Alternatively, make small parcel bags from pretty fabrics in any colours or patterns you like.

TALL TRIANGLES
I always enjoy looking through old magazines for photographs and illustrations to cover these boxes. I cut out red, paper berries with a hole puncher and glued them to the black and white design.

TIDY BUNDLE
A jewel-like, glazed fabric tied with a brilliant green bow makes ideal wrapping for a small present. If the gift is light enough, hang it from the boughs of the Christmas tree.

Corn yellow, paper ribbon

Violent pink, dried peony

MIRO CASKET
A reproduction of a Miró painting covers this attractive, casket-shaped, gift box.

Tile-look picture from a magazine

PATTERNED PYRAMIDS
Fill small, patterned pyramid boxes with sweets, truffles, or Turkish delight, to hang from the Christmas tree. If you need a hanging loop, thread a darning needle with ribbon or cord and pierce it through the top of the box. Tie the ribbon ends.

Riotous Colours

Liberally decorate and seal your boxed presents with bows (SEE PAGES 96–97). Ready-made square and rectangular boxes wrapped in gift papers demand matching or clashing ribbons, tapes, and strings. Let your imagination run wild with colours and textures because, at Christmas, anything goes.

Gilt, red ribbon

Gold-covered cord

Royal blue taffeta with a green sheen

Flower Decoration

A dried peony makes a flouncy centrepiece for the lid of this oval, store-bought box. Unrumple the petals of dried flowers by gently steaming them open. Use only a little steam from the spout of a kettle or the flower will collapse.

Christmas Wraps

FOLLOW THESE GIFT-WRAPPING techniques to give your carefully chosen presents the perfect finishing touch, before placing them under the tree.

✂ FABRIC WRAPPING ✂

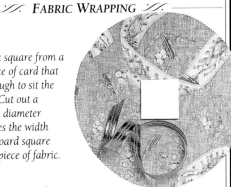

1 Cut out a square from a thick piece of card that is large enough to sit the present on. Cut out a circle with a diameter about 5 times the width of the cardboard square from a stiff piece of fabric.

2 Place the present on the card, then centre it on the fabric. Gather up the fabric in pleats, and tie firmly with a piece of ribbon to close the parcel. Attach a bow for a final flourish.

✂ PAPER WRAPPING ✂

1 Use paper long enough to wrap around the box, with a few centimetres' overlap. The paper's width should be 1½ times the width of the box. Secure one end of the paper to the top of the box with double-sided tape. Make a fold along the other end for a neat seam.

2 Bring the folded edge up over the top of the present and tape down. Next, seal the ends: just fold the top down, and tape to the box. Crease the folds formed by the top corners. Repeat for the other end.

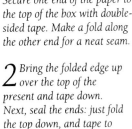

3 Fold both creased corners in against the box and tape down. Then, fold up the final flap and tape. Repeat on the other end.

FANCY BOWS

USE RIBBONS IN A MEDLEY of exciting materials and all the colours of the rainbow to make the most sumptuous bows. Tied and twisted into a myriad of brilliantly coloured loops and banners, bows add that final touch to Christmas trees, garlands, wreaths, and Christmas presents.

Prepare bows for the Christmas tree or for garlands well in advance, but it is best to tie your bows for presents after they have been wrapped, so that you can be sure that each bow matches its box.

Double bow in wire-edged, silver and blue ribbons

Single bow in gold-edged, red ribbon

SINGLE BOWS
Use one length of ribbon to make a single bow, with two pairs of overlapping loops, both twisted into figure-of-eights, and two trailing ends, neatened with diagonal cuts.

Single bow in mauve, metallic ribbon

Double bow in paper and striped, grosgrain ribbons

RIBBON-TYING METHODS

USE THE BASIC METHOD for single, double, and rosette bows. Keep loops open, and centres gathered tightly.

—— ///· **BASIC METHOD** ·/// ——

1 Unravel some of the ribbon and loop one end over the remainder. Hold in place with your thumb and forefinger.

2 With more ribbon, form the second loop of the bow, and bring the rest of the ribbon back over the top, to make an X-shape at the centre.

3 Now make a third loop, using more of the ribbon, and bringing the long end over the front of the bow.

4 Make another loop and bring the end back over the middle of the bow to make the second X-shape.

DOUBLE BOWS
Make a double bow with two or more ribbons, using the technique for a single bow. It is ideal for large presents.

MULTI-LOOP BOWS
Bows made with thin ribbon, string, or cord, look best if they have masses of loops and twirling ends.

Rosette bow in star-printed royal blue, silk ribbon

Rosette bow in pink- and wire-edged, green silk ribbon

• Multi-loop bow in loops of thin, pastel ribbon

Rosette bow in striped, silk ribbon

Multi-loop bow in metallic ribbons

Rosette bow in wire-edged, pink and orange, rainbow taffeta

ROSETTE BOWS
Create a rosette-like bow by continuing either the single or double ribbon-tying method, and forming several more loops. The finished ribbon has loops falling in all directions, and resembles a flower.

5 Pleat the centre of the bow with your fingers, working from the centre outwards, in both directions.

6 Secure the bow's centre with a length of thin wire or narrow ribbon. Open the loops and arrange the trailing ends.

·//· MULTI-LOOP BOW ·//·

1 Make several loops around your hand with a long piece of thin ribbon, string, or cord. Keep holding it while you remove your hand, then twist it in the centre to form a figure-of-eight.

2 Use another piece of the same ribbon and tie it in the centre, leaving long ends. Fan out the loops of the bow, and curl the trailing ends of ribbon by pulling them over a sharp knife.

TREE OF FLOWERS

IN A SENSE, a decorated Christmas tree is like a large flower arrangement. This thought inspired me to try covering a tree with flowers. The idea sounded glorious but, out of water, flowers have a short life. So, I arranged them in cellophane bags, pots, and baskets with water or wet foam. This way, the flowers last for a week or more.

WHAT YOU NEED
For a 1.8 m (6 ft) tree:
43 cm- (17 in-) diameter, fluted terracotta pot
2 strands white lights
3 bunches gypsophila
60 cornflowers
30 delphiniums
40 tulips
30 grape hyacinths
30 proteas
7 m (8 yd) smilax
40 anemones
20 mini-terracotta pots
15 small terracotta pots
30 small baskets
1 plastic bin liner
Six 23 x 11 x 8 cm (9 x 4½ x 3 in) wet foam bricks
Twenty 31 x 23 cm (12 x 9 in) cellophane squares
1 m (3 ft) tare ribbon
1 m (3 ft) gold cord

FLOWER BASKETS
Attach generous loops to the basket handles so that the flowers do not become entangled in the branches.

FRESH FLOWER POSIES
Cornflowers, gypsophila, and a tulip, wrapped in a water-filled cellophane cone and tied with a blue ribbon.

TERRACOTTA POTS
Glue cord to the rim of a flower-filled terracotta pot. Make a simple harness for the larger pots.

Smilax
Smilax is a delicate climber. Trim and place in a phial of water before garlanding.

Frosty Gypsophila
I have used gypsophila in all the arrangements on this Christmas tree. Its delicate, frosty, white flowers have a honey-like scent.

Miniature Arrangements

Choose light containers to hold your fresh flower arrangements. Once the baskets, pots, and cellophane are filled with water, they weigh considerably more.

Flower-filled Baskets & Pots

1 Measure and cut circles of plastic to line the inside of each container. The diameter of each circle should be twice the height plus the width of the base of the container. Wedge small cubes of soaked, wet foam in the containers to hold the lining.

2 Tie a loop of ribbon to the handle of each basket, and glue a loop of cord to the rim of each pot.

3 Push the stems of the flowers into the foam. Keep the arrangement low to prevent it from becoming top-heavy.

Cellophane-wrapped Flowers

1 Make a small bunch of flowers with stems 10 cm (4 in) long, removing all leaves from the lower halves of the stems. Place the flowers on a corner of a 31 x 23 cm (12 x 9 in) piece of clear cellophane.

2 Fold the cellophane up around the stems like an envelope. Fill with water and tie a ribbon around the cellophane, just below the flowerheads. Make a hanging loop by tying the ribbon ends. Hang to test for watertightness.

ROSEMARY & MIMOSA DESIGN

FOR PEOPLE WHO CELEBRATE CHRISTMAS in the cold and dark days of winter, it's pleasing to think that spring is not so far away. In the weeks before Christmas, shops are full of spring flowers: tulips, daffodils, hyacinths, and mimosa, as well as all the year-round favourites such as roses, lilies, and freesias. Of course, for those in the Southern hemisphere, the choice of flowers and foliage is always overwhelming at Christmas.

Take advantage of either the early spring or luscious summer flowers to create a sunny yellow arrangement for the holiday – it makes a welcome change from the traditional reds and greens. Here, I have arranged sweetly perfumed flowers in the shape of a miniature tree and a complementary swag. Although roses, ranunculus, dill, yellow peppers, and rosemary may seem an odd mix, their perfumes and shapes mingle deliciously, and they look as if they were always meant for each other.

Mimosa •

Dill •

Rose •

Miniature Tree
WHAT YOU NEED
*15 cm- (6 in-) diameter
plastic pot
18 cm- (7 in-) square
terracotta pot
Plaster of Paris mix
40 cm- (16 in-) long birch
branch
13 x 9 x 7.5 cm (5 x 3½ x 3 in)
wet foam block, soaked
40 cm- (16 in-) square
chicken wire
Mossing wire
45 sprigs mimosa
18 yellow roses
18 white ranunculus
12 stems flowering dill
5 handfuls bun moss*

METHOD
Place the plastic pot inside the terracotta pot. Pour wet plaster of Paris into the plastic pot. Push the branch into the wet plaster and prop it in position until the plaster sets. Carve a hole in the foam block so that it can perch on top of the branch. Cover with chicken wire, securing it with mossing wire. Arrange the flowers in the foam and cover the plaster of Paris with bun moss.

Swag
WHAT YOU NEED
*120 x 15 cm (4 ft x 6 in)
chicken wire
12 handfuls damp moss
70 sprigs mimosa
40 sprigs rosemary
24 yellow roses
20 stems flowering dill
15 clusters yellow peppers
Two 30 x 15 cm (12 x 6 in)
chicken wire
Mossing wire*

METHOD
Make a moss-filled roll with the longer piece of chicken wire and 8 handfuls of the damp moss (SEE PAGE 57, STEPS 1 AND 2). Shape the roll into 2 curves for the horizontal part of the swag. Using two-thirds of the plant material, stick the stems into the wire frame, starting from the ends and working to the middle. Make 2 smaller moss-filled rolls with the remaining chicken wire and moss, to form the vertical lengths of the swag. Insert the remaining flowers and foliage, working from the bottom to the top. Finish by securing the vertical pieces to the horizontal part of the swag with mossing wire.

Long-Lasting Swag

This sweet-smelling, golden swag would look lovely on a wall above a side table or mantelpiece. Make it as long or as tall as you wish. The swag will keep for months because, once you remove the roses, the other flowers and foliage slowly dry out, developing a softer, faded look.

Yellow pepper

Unripe, yellow pepper

Birch branch

Bun moss

Ranunculus

Rosemary

Flower Tree

The off-centred trunk of this miniature tree makes it look more interesting than if it were absolutely symmetrical. Keep the flowers fresh by putting a few ice cubes on top of the foam sphere each day.

TABLE CENTREPIECE

FLOWERS FROM ALL OVER THE WORLD are available at Christmas. This is the time to have the most wonderful combination of spring and summer varieties in a glorious riot of colour. I always try to use at least a touch of red in any festive arrangement. Here, every shade of that splendid colour, embracing bright and pale pinks, as well as oranges and ambers, is accounted for. Incorporate fruit, such as a few grapes or trails of dates, in an arrangement as well, to give any creation an added dimension. Another touch I like is to have a few petals or flowers scattered on the table beside the arrangement; if a flower falls, leave the petals where they lie. Finally, tailor the scale of the arrangement to the table, so that the flowers do not get in the way of the food or the guests.

Tulip

Carnation

Amaryllis

Eucalyptus

Euphorbia marginata

WHAT YOU NEED
Floral prong
Glass tazza or vase
Adhesive clay
13 x 9 x 7.5 cm (5 x 3½ x 3 in) wet foam block, soaked
Gold or silver spray paint, or silver moss
Stub wire
3 bunches grapes
20 poppies
15 carnations
10 sprigs eucalyptus foliage
10 tulips
8 nerines
7 snapdragons
6 Euphorbia marginata
5 stems 'La Reve' lilies
5 amaryllis
4 orchids

METHOD
Secure the prong in the tazza or vase with adhesive clay. Press the foam on to the prong (spray the sides of the bowl gold or silver, or line with silver moss to hide the foam.) Wire the grape bunches in first, then add the flowers one by one, so they look as if they are springing from the base of the bowl and cascading over the sides. For a peony-like effect, tie several carnations together, just below their flower-heads, and use them as one giant bloom.

Orchid

BOUNTEOUS DISPLAY
Bluey pinks, golden oranges, and glorious reds vie with each other to dazzle. Yet the overall effect is not overpowering; rather a fresh and subtle mélange of colours and shapes. The spicy fragrance of the ice-pink lilies is an added bonus.

Nerine

Snapdragon

Poppy

'La Reve' lily

Bunch of grapes

Last-minute Creations 104

Place Settings

A COMBINATION OF BEAUTIFUL FLOWERS and scented candles creates the perfect atmosphere for a memorable dinner party. Here, individual arrangements of flowers echo the table centrepiece, and some hold candles in their centres. Order your flowers well in advance, as most flower shops have sold their most beautiful specimens by Christmas Eve. Organize your time so that you can arrange the flowers at leisure the day before your party.

Individual Posies
Small, frosted glasses beside each place setting hold little posies made up of just a few flowers and foliage from the main arrangement.

'Paper White' narcissus

Freesia

Anemone

Agapanthus

Napkin Ring
WHAT YOU NEED
1 m (3 ft) wire-edged silver ribbon
Napkin
Silver thread
2 sprigs ivy
Glue
1 anemone flowerhead

METHOD
Cut the silver ribbon into a 25 cm- (10 in-) long piece and a 66 cm- (26 in-) long piece. Knot a loop in the shorter piece to hold the napkin, leaving long ends. From the longer ribbon, make a single bow (SEE PAGES 96–97) with 3 loops, and tie to the other ribbon with silver thread. Trim all the ribbon ends at a slant. About one hour before the meal, tie the ivy together with thread, leaving the ends long. Glue the anemone to the ivy spray, and attach to the silver bow with the thread.

Ranunculus •

Lilac •

MEDLEY OF FLOWERS
*A number of flowers, in shades of white,
yellow, pink, red, and lavender, are
arranged by colour, with trails of ivy
laced through them. Make sure that
some of the flowers are sweetly,
but not overpoweringly, scented.
If you make the centrepiece a
day in advance with very
fresh flowers, it should
last for six days
in a cool place.*

• 'Aladin' tulip

• Arum lily

'Mini Heron' ivy •

CANDLES IN POSIES
*Each subtlely scented bayberry
candle stands in a small, frosted
glass. Water fills the space
between the candle and
glass, to prolong the life
of the ruff of flowers.*

Carnation •

• Miniature rose

Table Trimmings

WHEN PREPARING FOR A SPECIAL Christmas dinner party, bear in mind that it is the extra trimmings that make a table look so marvellously welcoming. In addition to a beautiful flower centrepiece, delicate garlands of evergreens and berries encircling each plate are entrancing. You can also tie a posy of flowers to the back of each chair with a bow. This makes a delightful gift for each guest to take home at the end of the meal.

Prepare the floral centrepiece and chairback posies one day ahead, but attach them to the chairs only an hour before the party begins. Plate garlands can be time-consuming to prepare, so make them several hours in advance, and then store in a cool place. If you omit delicate-leaved foliage from the garlands, you can prepare them the day before.

Garland around a Plate
Use plant material in traditional Christmas colours to make a small garland for each place setting.

Variegated ivy

Douglas fir

Paper-ribbon bow

//.

Plate Garland
What You Need
Two 30 cm (12 in) stub wires
Gutta percha tape
20 sprigs Douglas fir
15 sprigs variegated, miniature-leaved ivy
10 berried sprigs cotoneaster or holly
Reel wire
Red, paper-ribbon bow
(SEE PAGES 96–97)
Matching ribbon
//.

Method
Twist the ends of the stub wires together to form a 60 cm (24 in) length. Cover with green, gutta percha tape. Starting from the left, attach plant material to the stub wire, using reel wire to secure. Allow the plant material to overlap, and cover the ends of each bunch with gutta percha tape. The greenery and berries look best if you use sprigs of varying lengths. Finish the garland with a festive bow, attached with a narrower piece of the same ribbon. Curl the wreath around the plate, leaving space at the front so that it does not prevent your guest from eating!

Spray of miniature green orchids

A modern, fluted vase
makes a perfect container for
an informal table centrepiece of
green orchids, red anemones,
perfumed roses, and Douglas
fir. Remember to keep the
arrangement low, so that
guests can see across the
table and talk to each
other with ease.

Anemone

Rose

Chairback Posy
WHAT YOU NEED
2 red anemones
3 red roses
2 sprays green, miniature
orchids
1 sprig ivy
4 sprigs Douglas fir
Reel wire
Red, paper-ribbon bow
(SEE PAGES 96–97)
Matching ribbon
Safety pins

METHOD
For each place
setting, make a
small, flat-backed
bouquet, binding the
stems together with
reel wire. Place in
water. An hour
before the party,
remove the bouquets
from water and dry the
stems. Tie the bow to the
front of the posy with thin
strips of the same ribbon. Leave
2 long ends to secure to the back of
the chair. If the chair is upholstered,
cut the ribbon ends shorter, and attach
the posy with 2 small safety pins.

Douglas
fir

Party Punches

PUNCHES ARE AS MUCH A PART OF CHRISTMAS as the tree and the cake. With a little attention to the decoration, they can look extra special. Anyone driving will appreciate light and refreshing non-alcoholic punches, such as the fruit cup flavoured with rosehips, citrus fruits, and grape juice. If you prefer some fizz, try the bubbly Champagne cup. I've also included some wickedly strong and rich drinks: an egg nog that's so thick it needs a spoon; a mulled claret that, to me, epitomizes Christmas; and a sophisticated peach-wine and Curaçao concoction.

Egg Nog
6 eggs (size 3), separated
85 g (3 oz) caster sugar
¼ tsp ground nutmeg
140 ml (5 fl oz) brandy or whisky
240 ml (8 fl oz) double cream
Ground nutmeg to decorate

Beat the egg yolks, sugar, and nutmeg. Add the alcohol and cream. Beat egg whites until stiff, and fold into the egg nog. Chill. Sprinkle with nutmeg. Serves 8.

Star fruit slice

Sugared, white grape

Champagne Cup

Sugared glass rim

Egg Nog

Mulled Claret

Kiwi fruit slice

Peach Punch

MULLED CLARET

475 ml (16 fl oz) water
5 cloves
4 allspice
½ cinnamon stick
Rind of 1 orange
2 tsp sugar
1 bottle claret
Twists of orange peel to
　decorate

Bring the water, spices,
and rind to the boil in a
large saucepan over a low
heat. Remove from the heat
and add the sugar. Leave for
30 minutes. Strain, then add
the wine. Heat to just below
boiling, and decorate with
orange peel. Serves 8.

PEACH PUNCH

2 bottles peach wine
105 ml (3½ fl oz) kirsch
105 ml (3½ fl oz) blue
　Curaçao
Juice of ½ lemon
2 white peaches, peeled and
　sliced, to decorate

Mix all the ingredients
together in a punch bowl,
and serve with slices of
peach floating on the
surface. Serves 15.

CHAMPAGNE CUP

2 bottles Champagne
740 ml (1¼ pt) soda water
210 ml (7 fl oz) Champagne
　brandy
1 tbs sugar
Sliced star fruit and kiwi fruit,
　and sugared, white grapes
　(SEE PAGES 82–83) to decorate

Thoroughly chill both the
Champagne and soda water.
Stir all the ingredients
together in a large punch
bowl. Decorate with the
sliced fruit and sugared
grapes. Serve immediately
to make the most of the
bubbles! Serves 15.

FRUIT CUP

140 g (5 oz) sugar
890 ml (1½ pt) each water,
　grape juice, and ginger ale
475 ml (16 fl oz) each
　redcurrant juice, strong
　hibiscus tea, and strong
　rosehip tea
Juice of 6 limes, 4 grapefruits,
　and 4 oranges
Crushed ice and fruit to
　decorate

Dissolve the sugar in the
water in a medium sauce-
pan over a low heat. When
cooled, pour the syrup into
a large punch bowl and add
the other ingredients. Chill.
When ready to serve, add
the crushed ice and decorate
with fruit, such as lychees,
redcurrants, slices of lime,
kumquat, or pomegranate.
Serves 30.

Pomegranate slice　Sliced limequat

Cluster of redcurrants

Fruit Cup

Sushi Buffet

THE JAPANESE HAVE A HIGH REGARD for both the taste and appearance of food. One of their most famous dishes, tantalizingly delicious and extremely decorative sushi, has become so popular that it is now available worldwide. For a festive gathering of family and friends, a buffet of sushi makes a very special and highly original feast. The delicate flavours provide just the change that the palate needs in a season when richness prevails. Do not be daunted if you have seen sushi chefs working at the speed of light. You will be able to produce the decorative dishes set out on these fans with ease. Most of the ingredients are readily available, although you may have to search for dried seaweed sheets. Substitute smoked salmon or trout for the seaweed, if you prefer.

SUSHI RICE
115 g (4 oz) short-grain, white rice
235 ml (8 fl oz) water
4–6 tbs icing sugar
4–6 tbs distilled malt vinegar
2 tbs ginger, finely chopped
2 tbs garlic, finely chopped

Place the rice and water in a covered saucepan and bring to the boil. Lower the heat to a simmer, and cook for 10–15 minutes, until the rice absorbs all the water, and is sticky. While the rice is hot, stir in the icing sugar, vinegar, ginger, and garlic. It is now ready for shaping into sushi.

Shell of soy sauce

French parsley

Salmon roe

Grated doiken (white radish)

Sushi Boats
Squeeze sushi rice into small ovals. Mist 20 x 4 cm (8 x 1½ in) strips of dried seaweed sheets, and fold in half, crossways. Shape around the rice, pinching the ends together (the damp seaweed will stick together). Fill with salmon roe or caviar.

Smoked Salmon Parcels
Place small squares of smoked salmon on individual pieces of plastic wrap. Roll sushi rice into little balls and place on top of the salmon. Twist the plastic wrap around the salmon and rice to form tight balls. Chill. When firm, unwrap the balls and garnish with wasabi or ginger paste, grated doiken, and edible leaves.

Red pepper julienne

FRESH GREENS IN SALMON
Humble green beans and spring
onions, wrapped in smoked
salmon, look and taste quite
delicious (SEE BELOW).

VEGETARIAN SUSHI
Baby corn-on-the-cob, green beans, and
red peppers nestle in sushi rice, and
are wrapped up in a sheet of sea-
weed (SEE BELOW). A garnish
of edible leaves and lemon
zest add to the colour.

Lemon zest

Wasabi paste

Ginger paste

SALMON & SEAWEED SLICES
A sheet of seaweed and marinated
salmon encircles sushi rice, green beans,
and baby carrots (SEE RIGHT). Serve with
condiments, such as horseradish and
mustard, and soy sauce in a shell.

METHOD FOR ROLLING SUSHI
This simple technique is quick to learn.
Fill the rolls with crunchy and colourful
ingredients. Place a 20 x 18 cm (8 x 7 in)
dried seaweed sheet on plastic wrap, shiny
side down. Mist with water to soften. Spread
sushi rice over the seaweed, leaving a 2.5 cm
(1 in) border on the 2 long sides. Place thin
strips of blanched vegetables or marinated fish
lengthways on the centre of the rice. Re-wet
the exposed seaweed, and carefully roll lengthways, using the plastic wrap to help you.
Chill until firm, then cut into 2.5 cm (1 in)
slices and remove the plastic wrap. Serve
with soy sauce and dabs of wasabi paste
and ginger paste. One roll makes 8 pieces.

MERINGUE YULE LOG

YULE WAS THE ANCIENT PAGAN FESTIVAL that celebrated the winter solstice. A feast prepared on the shortest day of the year preceded a period of celebrations, and the centrepiece of the festivities was a huge log for the fire, called the yule log. Modern cooks have made the log deliciously edible. Traditionally, it is a chocolate roulade covered and filled with a thick chocolate frosting. A scrumptious alternative is a frozen coffee and chocolate mousse cake covered with warm coffee meringue, the hot, toasted exterior and the frozen interior making a wonderful contrast. To get the timing right on this recipe, make the mousse cake first. While it is in the freezer, make the meringue mushrooms (they need to be cooked for 2 hours). Prepare the meringue for the log when you are ready to put the dessert in the oven. (This yule log should be eaten as soon as the meringue is cooked.)

WOODLAND SETTING
A woodland setting seemed the most natural decoration for a yule log. The dessert nestles in silvery moss strewn with a few berries, dried leaves, pine cones, and mushrooms made from meringue. To save time on the day, you can make the mousse cake and mushrooms up to two weeks in advance.

Autumn leaf

Pine cone

INGREDIENTS

Mousse Cake:
85 g (3 oz) butter
85 g (3 oz) caster sugar
3 eggs (size 3)
85 g (3 oz) cocoa powder
180 ml (6 fl oz) espresso coffee
60 g (2 oz) ground almonds
2 egg whites (size 3)

Meringue:
4 egg whites (size 3)
2 tsp instant coffee powder
¼ tsp cream of tartar
170 g (6 oz) icing sugar
60 g (2 oz) chocolate, melted
Cocoa powder for dusting

METHOD

Make the mousse cake. In a large bowl, beat the butter and sugar until creamy. Beat in the 3 whole eggs. In a small bowl, blend the cocoa powder and espresso coffee. Stir into the egg mixture with the ground almonds. Beat the 2 egg whites until stiff peaks form. Gently fold them into the egg mix. Line a 23 x 13 cm (9 x 5 in) baking tin with greased, greaseproof paper and pour in the mix. Bake at 175° C (350° F) for 30 minutes.

When the mousse cake has cooled, turn it on to a board and peel off the paper. Trim 2.5 cm (1 in) off one long side and freeze.

Make the meringue mushrooms. Beat one of the egg whites, ½ tsp of the instant coffee powder, and a pinch of the cream of tartar until soft peaks form. Sift in 45 g (1½ oz) of the icing sugar, and beat until stiff peaks form. Transfer the meringue to a piping bag with a 1.3 cm (½ in) nozzle. Pipe circles for the caps and lines for the stalks on to a baking tray covered with greaseproof paper. Bake at

95° C (200° F) for 2 hours. When cool, stick the stalks to the caps with melted chocolate. Dust them lightly with cocoa powder.

Prepare the meringue for the log, using the remaining egg whites, instant coffee powder, cream of tartar, and icing sugar, following the instructions above.

To assemble, place the frozen mousse cake on a baking tray and cover with the meringue. With a small knife, swirl it to make an attractive, bark-like texture and sculpt some broken branch ends. Bake at 220° C (425° F) for 8 minutes. Decorate the yule log, and serve immediately. Serves 8.

Meringue mushroom

Silver moss

Rowan berry

FRUIT SAVARIN

IF YOU ARE SEARCHING for an absolutely spectacular dessert, then look
no further. This delectable ring of leavened cake is drenched in rum
syrup and overflowing with luscious, sticky, poached and preserved
fruits. Fresh fruit and sprigs of sugared mint leaves and flowers add
a final decorative flourish. The savarin looks so amazing that it
seems a pity to make the first cut and dismantle
it. However, once that first step is over, it should
be easy to persuade guests to try a piece! This
dessert has so many different flavours and textures
to be shared and enjoyed: pears, figs, apricots, cherries,
oranges, nuts, and profiteroles. Add them to the most
moist cake imaginable and you can be sure that
Fruit Savarin will become a Christmas regular.

Wine-poached Pear

Fresh fig

FRUIT SAVARIN
Cake:
15 g (½ oz) fresh yeast
4 tbs sugar
295 ml (½ pt) lukewarm milk
455 g (1 lb) strong white flour
1 tsp salt
6 eggs (size 2), at room temperature
170 g (6 oz) melted butter
Syrup:
590 ml (1 pt) water
455 g (1 lb) caster sugar
210 ml (7 fl oz) rum or kirsch
Decorations:
Wine-poached Pears (RIGHT)
Fresh fruit
Crystallized fruit (SEE
  PAGES 38–39)
Sugared flowers and mint leaves (SEE PAGES 82–83)
Caramel profiteroles and nuts (SEE PAGE 89)

Combine the yeast, sugar,
and milk. Sift in the flour
and salt, then beat in the
eggs. Place in an oiled bowl,
cover, and let rise in a warm
place for 1 hour, until
doubled in size. Punch down
and mix in the melted butter.
Stir vigorously for 7 minutes,
until smooth and elastic.
Butter and flour a 31 cm
(12 in) savarin mould, and
pour in the batter. Cover and
let rise in a warm place for
45 minutes. Bake at 190° C
(375° F) for 35
minutes. Cover loosely
with foil if it starts to
brown too much.

Meanwhile, make the syrup.
Vigorously boil the water and
sugar for 20 minutes, until syrupy.
After 5 minutes, add the rum or kirsch.

Remove the savarin from the oven and,
after a few minutes, shake to loosen in its
tin. Prick with a skewer, then pour half of
the hot syrup over. When cold, turn on to
a 46 cm (18 in) plate, fill with fruit, and
decorate. Serve the remaining syrup
separately. Serves 16.

Crystallized
pear half

Caramel nut

Fresh clementine

Caramel
profiterole

WINE-POACHED PEARS
1 bottle Beaujolais
455 g (16 oz) sugar
6 whole cloves
10 medium, firm pears
3 drops natural, red food
*   colouring*
3 tbs créme de mûre
*   (blackberry liqueur) or*
*   créme de cassis*

Bring the wine, sugar, and
cloves to boil in a large
saucepan, then reduce to
a simmer. Peel the pears
(leaving the stems on), and
immediately place them in
the syrup. Simmer for about
15–20 minutes, until the
pears are translucent and
just tender. When cool, add
the food colouring and
alcohol. Leave overnight.
Remove the pears, and boil
the syrup to reduce by a
third. Spoon the syrup over
the pears to glaze.

Crystallized
orange slice

Crystallized
cherry

FRUITY FEAST
A sumptuous, rum-soaked
savarin heaped with
decorative fruits makes a
breath-taking dessert for
Christmas Day dinner.
Guests can help themselves
to their favourite fruits.

Sugared primrose

Sugared
mint leaf

Crystallized
apricot

TEMPLATES

ENLARGE THESE TEMPLATES to the size you require on a photocopier.
Use the enlarged image to give you an outline.

CHRISTMAS CHAINS

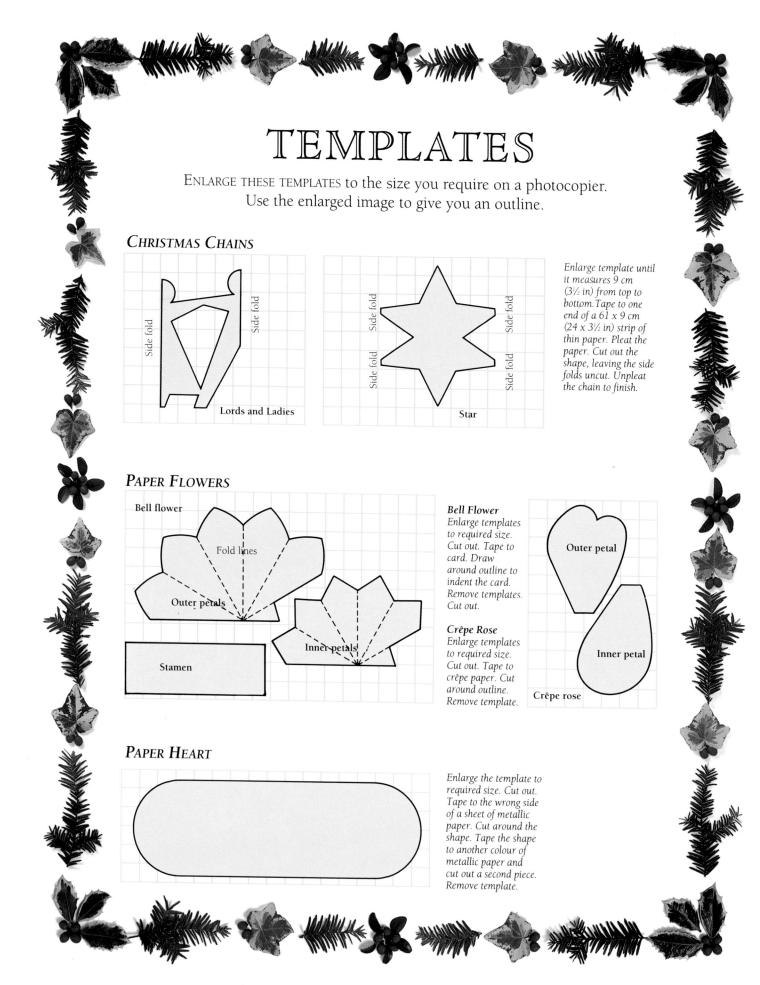

Side fold

Side fold

Lords and Ladies

Side fold

Side fold

Side fold

Side fold

Star

Enlarge template until it measures 9 cm (3½ in) from top to bottom. Tape to one end of a 61 x 9 cm (24 x 3½ in) strip of thin paper. Pleat the paper. Cut out the shape, leaving the side folds uncut. Unpleat the chain to finish.

PAPER FLOWERS

Bell flower

Fold lines

Outer petals

Stamen

Inner petals

Outer petal

Inner petal

Crêpe rose

Bell Flower
Enlarge templates to required size. Cut out. Tape to card. Draw around outline to indent the card. Remove templates. Cut out.

Crêpe Rose
Enlarge templates to required size. Cut out. Tape to crêpe paper. Cut around outline. Remove template.

PAPER HEART

Enlarge the template to required size. Cut out. Tape to the wrong side of a sheet of metallic paper. Cut around the shape. Tape the shape to another colour of metallic paper and cut out a second piece. Remove template.

GIFT BOXES

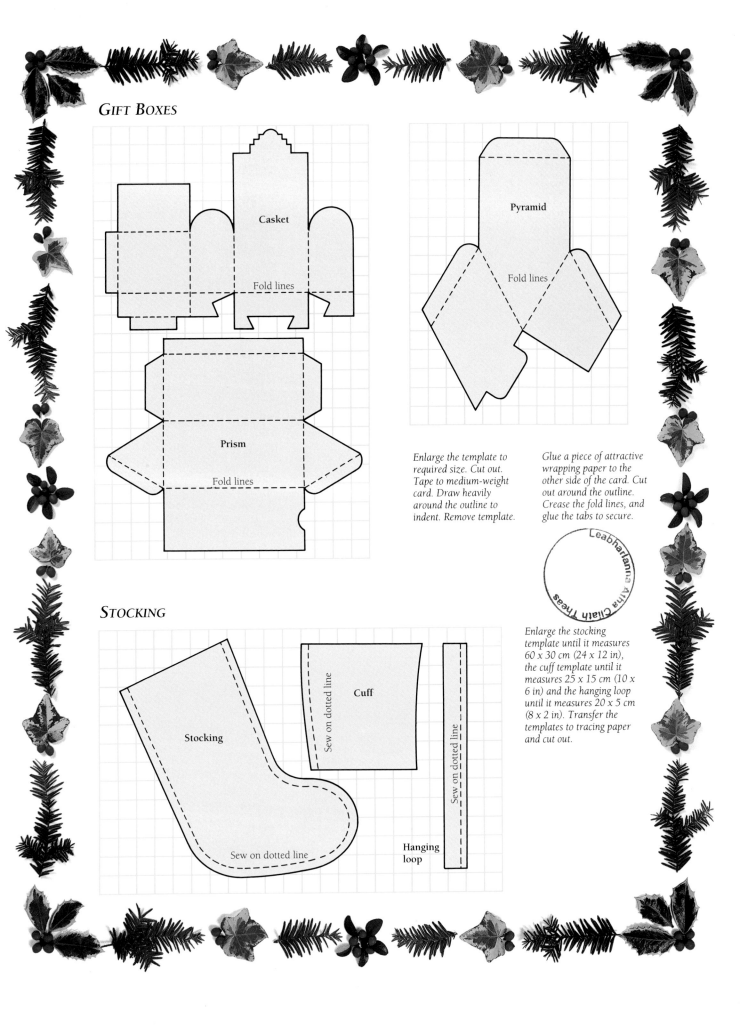

Casket

Fold lines

Pyramid

Fold lines

Prism

Fold lines

Enlarge the template to required size. Cut out. Tape to medium-weight card. Draw heavily around the outline to indent. Remove template.

Glue a piece of attractive wrapping paper to the other side of the card. Cut out around the outline. Crease the fold lines, and glue the tabs to secure.

STOCKING

Stocking

Sew on dotted line

Cuff

Sew on dotted line

Sew on dotted line

Hanging loop

Enlarge the stocking template until it measures 60 x 30 cm (24 x 12 in), the cuff template until it measures 25 x 15 cm (10 x 6 in) and the hanging loop until it measures 20 x 5 cm (8 x 2 in). Transfer the templates to tracing paper and cut out.

INDEX

ACKNOWLEDGMENTS

The author would like to thank the following people for
their help on *Malcolm Hillier's Christmas*: Quentin Roake for all his
help in creating this book, Michael Handford for supplying antiques,
the Conran Shop for props; Gisela Graham for decorations, Jo Scott
Douglas for dried flowers, Mr and Mrs O D Boraston for antique jelly
moulds, Ken Vincent from Terracotta UK for containers for the trees,
John Austin for flowers, Anta for tartan fabrics, Harry the lurcher
who slept through most of it, and Frank the cat who slept
through all of it.

Dorling Kindersley would like to thank Belinda Whitworth for
compiling the index, Angeles Gavira, Helen Townsend, Belinda
Whitworth, Edel Brosman, and Andrea Fair for editorial help; Claire
Pegrum, Ann Thompson, and Kevin Ryan for design help; Janos Marffy
for template artwork and air-brushing, Alastair Wardle for computer
assistance, Clare Ferguson for preparing food for photography, Ailsa
Cruickshank and Lucy Offer for additional food preparation,
and James Knapp for assisting Diana Miller
with photography.

All photographs by Diana Miller, except: p 36–37 and step-by-step
photographs 67, 96–97 Matthew Ward; and border photograph
p 4–7, 116–120 Sue Atkinson.